A Conceptual Framework for Lake Michigan Coastal/Nearshore Ecosystems, With Application to Lake Michigan Lakewide Management Plan (LaMP) Objectives

By Paul W. Seelbach, Lisa R. Fogarty, David Bo Bunnell, Sheridan K. Haack, and Mark W. Rogers

Open-File Report 2013–1138

U.S. Department of the Interior
U.S. Geological Survey

U.S. Department of the Interior
SALLY JEWELL, Secretary

U.S. Geological Survey
Suzette M. Kimball, Acting Director

U.S. Geological Survey, Reston, Virginia: 2013

For more information on the USGS—the Federal source for science about the Earth, its natural and living resources, natural hazards, and the environment, visit http://www.usgs.gov or call 1–888–ASK–USGS.

For an overview of USGS information products, including maps, imagery, and publications,
visit http://www.usgs.gov/pubprod

To order this and other USGS information products, visit http://store.usgs.gov

Contents

Abstract..1

Introduction...1

    An Ecosystem- and Process-Based Conceptual Framework to Support
        Great Lakes Resource Management Programs...2

    Applying the Framework to Lake Michigan Lakewide Management Plan Goals...................5

    References...5

We Can All Eat the Fish...6

    Importance of Fish Consumption to Lake Michigan Communities.................................6

    Contaminants, Sources, and Risks...6

    Fish Consumption Advisories and Monitoring..7

    Contaminant Trends...7

    Identifying Key Processes and Uncertainties...7

        Geomorphic Processes...7

        Hydrologic Processes..8

        Biological Processes...9

    What We Know from Monitoring Efforts..9

    Examples of Knowledge Gaps..9

    References...10

We Can All Drink the Water...12

    Importance of Drinking Water to Lake Michigan Communities....................................12

    Drinking-Water Monitoring...12

    Identifying Key Processes and Uncertainties...13

        Geomorphic Processes...13

        Hydrologic Processes..13

        Biological Processes...14

    What We Know from Monitoring Efforts..14

    Knowledge Gaps and Uncertainties..15

    References...15

We Can All Swim in the Water...17

    Importance of Swimming in the Water to Lake Michigan Communities.......................17

    Beach Monitoring..17

    Identifying Key Processes and Uncertainties...18

        Geomorphic Processes...18

        Hydrologic Processes..18

        Biological Processes...18

    What We Know From Monitoring Efforts...19

    Knowledge Gaps and Uncertainties..19

    References...20

All Habitats Are Healthy, Naturally Diverse, and Sufficient to Sustain Viable Biological
        Communities...22

    Importance of Healthy Habitats...22

    Habitats and Their Structure...22

    Habitat Trends...23

All Habitats Are Healthy, Naturally Diverse, and Sufficient to Sustain Viable Biological Communities (*continued*)

    Identifying Key Processes and Uncertainty 23

        Geomorphic Processes 23

        Hydrologic Processes...24

        Biological Processes 24

    What We Know from Monitoring Efforts..25

        Knowledge Gaps..25

    References...25

Figures

    1. Diagram of the proposed conceptual framework intended to support an ecosystem- and process-based approach to attaining the goals of the Lake Michigan Lakewide Management Plan (LaMP).............................3

Tables

    1. Matrix of the primary ecosystem disciplines whose processes drive ecological structure and function within each of the primary aquatic zones that together constitute the Great Lakes ecosystem, and the key processes that fall within each zone 4

Appendixes

Processes and components that impact the Great Lakes Lakewide Management Plan goal—

    1. We Can All Eat the Fish...28

    2. We Can All Drink the Water...30

    3. We Can All Swim in the Water. 32

    4. All Habitats are Healthy, Naturally Diverse, and Sufficient To Sustain Viable Biological Communities..34

Abbreviations and Acronyms

AOC	Areas of Concern
BEACH	Beaches Environmental Assessment and Coastal Health Act of 2000
CCL	Contaminant Candidate List
DDT	dichlorodiphenyltrichloroethane
EPA	U.S. Environmental Protection Agency
FCAs	fish consumption advisories
FIB	fecal indicator bacteria
GLNPO	Great Lakes National Program Office (EPA)
GLFMP	Great Lakes Fish Monitoring Program
GLRI	Great Lakes Restoration Initiative
HAB	harmful algal bloom
HGM	hydro-geomorphic
LaMP	Lakewide Management Plan
NOAA	National Oceanic and Atmospheric Administration
PBBs	polybrominated biphenyls
PBDEs	polybrominated diphenyl ethers
PCBs	polychlorinated biphenyls
qPCR	quantitative polymerase chain reaction
SOLEC	State of the Lakes Ecosystem Conference
USGS	U.S. Geological Survey

A Conceptual Framework for Lake Michigan Coastal/ Nearshore Ecosystems, With Application to Lake Michigan Lakewide Management Plan (LaMP) Objectives

By Paul W. Seelbach,[1] Lisa R. Fogarty,[2] David Bo Bunnell,[1] Sheridan K. Haack,[2] and Mark W. Rogers[1]

Abstract

The Lakewide Management Plans (LaMPs) within the Great Lakes region are examples of broad-scale, collaborative resource-management efforts that require a sound ecosystems approach. Yet, the LaMP process is lacking a holistic framework that allows these individual actions to be planned and understood within the broader context of the Great Lakes ecosystem. In this paper we (1) introduce a conceptual framework that unifies ideas and language among Great Lakes managers and scientists, whose focus areas range from tributary watersheds to open-lake waters, and (2) illustrate how the framework can be used to outline the geomorphic, hydrologic biological, and societal processes that underlie several goals of the Lake Michigan LaMP, thus providing a holistic and fairly comprehensive roadmap for tackling these challenges. For each selected goal, we developed a matrix that identifies the key ecosystem processes within the cell for each lake zone and each discipline; we then provide one example where a process is poorly understood and a second where a process is understood, but its impact or importance is unclear. Implicit in these objectives was our intention to highlight the importance of the Great Lakes coastal/nearshore zone. Although the coastal/nearshore zone is the important linkage zone between the watershed and open-lake zones—and is the zone where most LaMP issues are focused—scientists and managers have a relatively poor understanding of how the coastal/nearshore zone functions. We envision follow-up steps including (1) collaborative development of a more detailed and more complete conceptual model of how (and where) identified processes are thought to function, and (2) a subsequent gap analysis of science and monitoring priorities.

---

[1] U.S. Geological Survey, Great Lakes Science Center.

[2] U.S. Geological Survey, Michigan Water Science Center.

Introduction

It is now broadly recognized that Great Lakes resource management programs must be based on an ecosystems approach. Such a holistic, systems-level approach identifies key driving processes that operate at different, often hierarchical, scales to influence selected ecosystem characteristics; for example, processes that sustain healthy and interconnected aquatic habitat mosaics. The Lakewide Management Plans (LaMPs) within the Great Lakes region are examples of broadscale, collaborative resource management efforts that require a sound ecosystems approach. Each LaMP has different endpoint goals, against which progress can be measured through time as specific management actions are implemented in selected areas by particular agencies. Yet, the LaMP process currently lacks a holistic framework that allows these individual actions to be planned and understood within the broader context of the Great Lakes ecosystem. This paper addresses two objectives that are meant to introduce and illustrate the use of an ecosystem-based framework for regional-scale resource management.

Our first objective is to introduce a conceptual framework that unifies ideas and language among Great Lakes managers and scientists, whose focus areas range from watersheds to open-lake waters. Our conceptual framework builds upon previous works, such as (1) the Coastal Habitat Classification Framework of the U.S. Geological Survey (USGS), Aquatic GAP Analysis Program (U.S. Geological Survey, 2013); (2) the U.S. Environmental Protection Agency (EPA) framework for "Assessing and Reporting on Ecological Conditions" (U.S. Environmental Protection Agency, 2002); and (3) the EPA "Conceptual Model of the Relationships Between Ecosystem Health, Stressors, and Sources of Stress" (Environment Canada and U.S. Environmental Protection Agency, 1997). The framework is a matrix that organizes driving ecosystem processes by aquatic eco-zones and key ecological disciplines (fig. 1).

Our second objective builds on the first, in that we seek to illustrate how the framework can be used to outline the geomorphic, hydrologic, biological, and societal processes that underlie several goals of the Lake Michigan LaMP, thus providing a holistic and fairly comprehensive roadmap for addressing these goals. In this paper, we use four of the six Lake Michigan LaMP goals as examples of using this framework to address key Great Lakes ecosystem issues. The goals we focus on are the following:

1. "We can all eat the fish."

2. "We can all drink the water."

3. "We can all swim in the water."

4. "All habitats are healthy, naturally diverse, and sufficient to sustain viable biological communities."

For each goal, we developed a matrix that identifies the key ecosystem processes within the cell for each lake zone and each discipline; we then provided one example where a process is poorly understood and a second where a process is understood, but its impact or importance is unclear. These examples are meant to be illustrative because we hope to stimulate more formalized expert- and partner-driven matrix development, project synthesis, and gap analysis in the future.

Implicit in these objectives was our intention to highlight the importance of the Great Lakes coastal/nearshore zone. Although the coastal/nearshore zone is the important linkage zone between watershed and open-lake zones, scientists and managers have a relatively poor understanding of how the coastal/nearshore zone functions. This zone is the basin focus of (1) accumulation and chemical transformation of many human-derived loads, such as agricultural runoff, industrial waste, and urban storm and sewer outflows; (2) human economic uses of the Great Lakes, such as commercial harbors, water supply for industry and municipalities, and waste disposal; and (3) human enjoyment of the Great Lakes, such as for swimming, fishing, recreational boating, and viewing. Largely because of the diversity of habitats in this transitional zone between river and lake—including lowland rivers and their flood-plain wetlands, drowned-river-mouth lakes and embayments, deltaic wetlands, river plumes, and coastal wetlands—the coastal/nearshore zone is a productive biological hot spot where many Great Lakes fauna spend at least part of their life history. Finally, the coastal/nearshore zone is where most of the LaMP endpoint goals are measured.

Our overall goal for this report is to help frame Lake Michigan management efforts under a unifying, ecosystem-based conceptual framework, where key processes underlying each endpoint goal will be explicitly considered.

An Ecosystem- and Process-Based Conceptual Framework to Support Great Lakes Resource Management Programs

The conceptual ecological framework presented in this paper is a simple, but holistic, approach for identifying the processes critical to effective Great Lakes resource management. Because these inland seas are daunting in size and complexity, many aspects of the lake ecosystem have traditionally been studied and managed as local and narrowly focused issues, independent of other potentially related aspects—and some aspects have received little attention.

The first major element of this conceptual framework outlines three geographic zones: the *watershed, coastal/nearshore,* and *open lake;* and the second major element identifies the key *geomorphic, hydrologic, biological,* and *societal* processes that occur within each zone (fig. 1). We chose not to apply strict criteria to delineating the three zones, largely because in nature there are no simple and abrupt demarcations among these habitats. Thus, our framework embraces the inherent variation among zones and processes across Lake Michigan's complex ecosystem. In simple terms, *watershed* includes the terrestrial drainage area surrounding the tributaries, *open lake* reflects waters deeper than 30 meters (m) or the depth at which the thermocline intersects the bottom of the lake, and *coastal/nearshore* represents the diverse habitats in between the watershed and the open-lake zones. Each of these zones is commonly studied and managed; however, each also transitions into, and thus influences, system processes in the adjacent zone. These areas of intersection and mixing are difficult to study, but they often are most critical to biological processes of interest. Instead of viewing these geographic zones as separate arenas, this framework highlights the importance of interconnections between them and the resulting influences on system processes and related ecological characteristics.

The second major element represents important disciplinary subsystems within each geographic zone in the larger lake ecosystem. We use these major ecosystem disciplines to organize the process subsystems, which can be viewed as parallels to the human body's subsystems; for example, the circulatory system.

Hydrologic processes circulate or move water, sediments, nutrients, and other materials into and through the zones. Watershed hydrology involves catchment-specific water budgets, as well as alternate flow routing via evapotranspiration, surface waters, or groundwater paths. Coastal/nearshore hydrology has been little studied, involving complexities of river- and lake-water mixing, lake seiche regimes, lake upwellings, and nearshore-current dynamics. Open-lake hydrology involves major water circulation patterns and

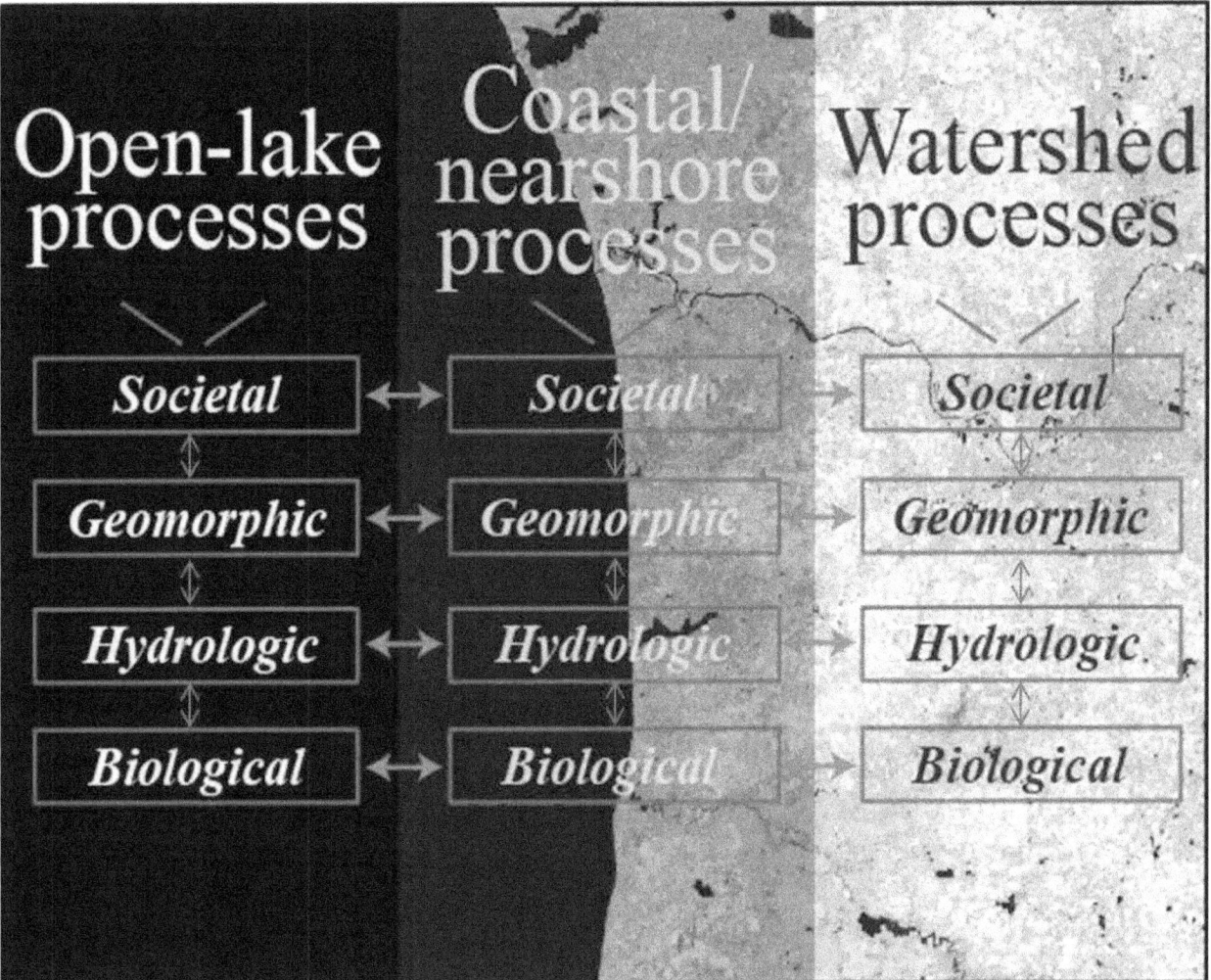

Figure 1. The proposed conceptual framework is intended to support an ecosystem- and process-based approach to attaining the goals of the Lake Michigan Lakewide Management Plan (LaMP). Building a detailed understanding of the geomorphic, hydrologic, and biological processes within the open lake, coastal/nearshore, and watershed ecosystem zones helps determine LaMP progress relative to specific management goals. In addition, societal values in each of the geographic lake zones weigh heavily in resource management decisions. The coastal/nearshore zone serves as the linkage (as orange arrows indicate) among the three habitats. Climate, geology, and the legacy human footprint are the overriding processes that influence all lake-zone processes at an ecosystem-wide scale.

seasonal stratification of layers of water with different temperatures. Water characteristics such as nutrient concentrations or temperature are included under this "hydrologic" heading.

Geomorphic processes include historical processes that have shaped the form and texture of the local landscape; current processes of sediment erosion, transport, and deposition; and patterns that influence local habitat character. Geomorphic processes influence numerous resource management issues, such as contaminant sources and dynamics. The characteristics of aquatic habitat are largely shaped by hydrologic and geomorphic processes, which are often referred to in wetland and stream ecology as hydro-geomorphic or "HGM" drivers. Peterson (2003) clarified that aquatic habitats generally include both "static" aspects (the local, historical geomorphic setting) and overlying "dynamic" aspects (the hydrologic and present-day geomorphic processes).

Biological processes include fundamental nutrient and biogeochemical cycles governed by the ecology and activity of microorganisms, trophic energy (or food web) dynamics, and sometimes the presence of biological structure, such as aquatic plants or macrophytes. Biological processes overlay, and are driven and constrained by, the spatial physical template created by the HGM processes.

Finally, we recognize the important influence of *societal processes* on the ecosystem as well, because societal perspectives and values that are in play at local and regional scales will determine the cost/benefit tradeoffs that ultimately drive resource management decisions.

The geomorphic, hydrologic, and biological system processes all have natural characteristics that provide the basis for understanding that disciplinary subsystem, and each has then been changed, to some degree, by human actions within each of the three geographic zones. Thus, within each discipline-zone cell of the framework matrix, we further stratify processes as "natural" or "anthropogenic." And we recognize that these human-influenced processes will often have ramifications across multiple zones or multiple disciplines.

The resulting ecological zone-discipline matrix allows us to examine selected topics, programs, and endpoints from a holistic, systems perspective. To examine each selected issue, a table based on the matrix template was built to identify specific, key driving processes that lie within each of the matrix cells, because often the issues that are observed or measured within a particular cell are in fact driven by processes in other cells. The resulting table (the general case shown in table 1) is a conceptual model of how the lake ecosystem works across space and disciplines to influence the issue of interest. Our framework is, at minimum, a sort of checklist reminding the user not to overlook processes in other lake zones or disciplines. The framework can be used to map and assess current or proposed science and management programs, and the results could then be used to identify program gaps or strategic directions.

To begin to address the Lake Michigan ecosystem by means of a more holistic approach, we used the conceptual framework to develop a coarse outline of system processes important to several Lake Michigan LaMP goals. Examples of both natural and anthropogenic processes are identified in tables similar to table 1 (appendixes 1–4). We envision follow-up steps including (1) collaborative development of a more detailed and more complete conceptual model of how (and where) the identified processes are thought to function and (2) a subsequent gap analysis of science and monitoring needs. The gap analysis would establish priorities for subsequent science and monitoring efforts, adaptively moving us towards improved lake management.

The intention of this framework is to encourage viewing the lake ecosystem as a system of multidiscipline processes that operate within and across different geographic areas. The focus of the framework is on the interacting processes and the need to understand the influence they have on reaching desired endpoints or causing undesirable results. With this framework, we hope to assist programs within the Great Lakes region to identify science and monitoring strengths and weaknesses, thus providing more complete information for making management decisions and prioritizing future research needs.

Table 1.   Matrix of the primary ecosystem disciplines whose processes drive ecological structure and function within each of the primary aquatic zones that together constitute the Great Lakes ecosystem, and the key processes that fall within each zone.

Primary ecosystem disciplines	Open lake	Coastal/nearshore	Watershed
Societal	*Key processes*	*Key processes*	*Key processes*
Biological	*Key processes*	*Key processes*	*Key processes*
Hydrologic	*Key processes*	*Key processes*	*Key processes*
Geomorphic	*Key processes*	*Key processes*	*Key processes*

Applying the Framework to Lake Michigan Lakewide Management Plan Goals

The proposed conceptual framework was used to develop a process matrix to address four of the Lake Michigan LaMP goals: (1) we can all eat the fish, (2) we can all drink the water, (3) we can all swim in the water, and (4) all habitats are healthy, naturally diverse, and sufficient to sustain viable biological communities. Each of the following chapters briefly describes how the proposed conceptual framework can be used to support an ecosystem- and process-based management program and includes a table (as an appendix) of example processes critical for each LaMP goal. We offer the caveat that although we clearly recognize the importance of societal processes within the ecosystem scheme, we did not discuss these in the example chapters because our authorship lacked this expertise. We envision the conceptualization of societal process as part of the "subsequent steps" described above.

References

Environment Canada and U.S. Environmental Protection Agency, 1997, State of the Great Lakes, 1997—The year of the nearshore: Chicago, Ill., Great Lakes National Program Office, EPA 905-R-97-013, 76 p.

Peterson, M.S., 2003, A conceptual view of environment-habitat production linkages in tidal river estuaries: Reviews in Fisheries Science, v. 11, no. 4, p. 291–313.

U.S. Environmental Protection Agency, 2002, A framework for assessing and reporting on ecological condition—An SAB report: Washington, D.C., EPA-SAB-EPEC-02-009 [variously paged].

U.S. Geological Survey, 2013, Coastal aquatic GAP analysis Web site, accessed March 19, 2013, at *http://www.glsc.usgs.gov/main.php?content=research_GAP_coastal&title=Aquatic%20GAP0&menu=research_NCE_GAP*.

Rainbow smelt, Minnesota Sea Grant

We Can All Eat the Fish

Importance of Fish Consumption to Lake Michigan Communities

Over 30 percent of global fish production is in freshwater systems (Food and Agriculture Organization of the United Nations, 2010), and wild fish harvesting provides an important protein source for humans (Welcomme and others, 2010). Consuming harvested wild fish provides multiple health benefits, because fish are a good source of protein and are typically low in saturated fat (Gebhardt and Thomas, 2002). Estimated lakewide fish harvests in Lake Michigan have exceeded 19 tons per year in recent decades (Brian Briedert, Indiana Department of Natural Resources, unpublished data); however, fish consumption advisories (FCAs) have been issued for all commercially and recreationally harvested fish species from Lake Michigan, except alewife (*Alosa pseudoharengus*). Alewife is not considered a food fish, but it is used as a protein source in livestock and aquaculture feeds, thus providing an indirect pathway for human consumption.

Fish consumption can be a major source of human exposure to carcinogenic and toxicological contaminants (Sidhu, 2003) including methylmercury, polychlorinated biphenyls (PCBs), and organic pesticides and herbicides such as chlordane and dichlorodiphenyltrichloroethane (DDT). Contaminants of increasing concern include polybrominated biphenyls (PBBs) and polybrominated diphenyl ethers (PBDEs) and pharmaceuticals including chemicals that interfere with the body's hormone system (endocrine disruptors), personal care products, and prescription drugs. Nevertheless, relationships between fish consumption and human health risks from these emergent contaminants are not understood well enough at the present time to invoke FCAs.

Contaminants, Sources, and Risks

Mercury is a natural element released from processes such as volcanic eruptions and human activities such as the burning of fossil fuels. Bacteria convert mercury to an organic form in water, methylmercury, which can bioaccumulate within food webs. Methylmercury accumulates within fish muscle and causes neurological impairment to humans who consume the fish (Goyer and others, 2000). Similar to mercury, PCBs bioaccumulate within food webs and become concentrated in the lipids and tissues of top fish-eating carnivores or slow-growing fish that live near the bottom of the lake. PCBs had multiple industrial uses and were banned in 1979, because they have been suggested as a carcinogen and a cause of birth defects in humans (Mozaffarian and Rimm, 2006). Many FCAs are targeted towards limiting consumption of fish species with the high potential of PCB bioaccumulation by sensitive population groups such as young children, pregnant women, or women of childbearing age. A large group of organic chemicals identified as chemicals of emerging concern (CECs) also have been detected in Great Lakes surface waters, bottom sediments, and wastewaters entering the lakes (Lee and others, 2012). Among these CECs are PBDEs, which stem primarily from manufactured flame retardant chemicals commonly used in building materials and have characteristics similar to PCBs, whereas pharmaceuticals can disrupt hormone production and control in humans.

Fish Consumption Advisories and Monitoring

Individual States and tribal entities are responsible for setting their own FCAs. Within the Great Lakes, the Great Lakes Sport Fish Consumption Advisory Task Force facilitates determination of FCAs and includes members from public health and natural resource agencies from each of the eight States bordering the Great Lakes, along with representatives from the EPA, Native American tribes, and Canadian agencies. FCAs originally were compared with risk standards developed by the Food and Drug Administration; however, the potential for increased consumption of contaminated fish by anglers relative to nonanglers resulted in modification of FCAs to decrease health risks to anglers. New advisories are based on cancer, reproductive, and developmental risks. Protocols have been developed by the Great Lakes Sport Fish Consumption Advisory Task Force to suggest consistent approaches for determining mercury- and PCB-driven FCAs across the Great Lakes.

Monitoring for determining "We can all eat the fish" relies primarily upon sampling of whole fish and fish flesh. The Great Lakes Fish Monitoring Program (GLFMP) within the Environmental Protection Agency Great Lakes National Program Office (EPA GLNPO) monitors bioaccumulative organic compounds in Lake Michigan by using lake trout (*Salvelinus namaycush*) as a biological monitor of contaminants in the open-lake area and Chinook and Coho salmon (*Oncorhynchus tshawytscha* and *O. kisutch*, respectively) for monitoring game fish fillets. The open lake has historically been sampled offshore at three sites that were selected to minimize nearshore influences: Saugatuck, Charlevoix, and Sturgeon Bay, Michigan. Game fish fillet monitoring by the GLFMP relies upon contaminant samples provided by States. Coho salmon are analyzed in even years, and Chinook salmon are analyzed in odd years. Game fish are sampled at approximately 10 rivermouths around the lake, and adults are targeted prior to spawning. The GLFMP also samples for contaminants in the water column and sediments. The EPA GLNPO and the Sport Fish Contaminant Monitoring Program in Ontario have collectively monitored contaminants in fish for over 3 decades. Individual States often do additional sampling of other Lake Michigan fish species that are important to their constituents and their consumption preferences. For example, the Michigan Department of Natural Resources has tested for contaminants in 21 species since the mid-1980s; however, Chinook and Coho salmon and lake trout are the most continuously and regularly monitored species (Michigan Department of Natural Resources, unpublished data).

Contaminant Trends

The 2009 "Nearshore Areas of the Great Lakes" report (U.S. Environmental Protection Agency and Environment Canada, 2009) determined the status of Lake Michigan contaminants in game fish as "fair" with an improving trend. Ongoing monitoring by the GLFMP and its partner State agencies has generally shown that contaminant levels in game fish have decreased since monitoring programs began, yet contaminant levels are still above levels requiring FCAs. For example, decreasing DDT and PCB concentrations in lake trout from the early 1970s to 2003 were reported by Carlson and others (2010), who also reported changes in first-order rate constants for multiple contaminants in lake trout that resulted in increased half-lives of contaminants between the mid-1970s and late-1990s. Carlson and others (2010) concluded that Lake Michigan contaminants may have reached stable concentrations and will persist within the Lake Michigan ecosystem for future decades. Persistence of contaminants within the ecosystem may be caused by internal recycling within the water near the lake bottom (Jeremiason and others, 1998).

Identifying Key Processes and Uncertainties

Monitoring programs for fish contaminants have focused on endpoint metrics, such as mercury concentration per meal portion, and an important next step is to better understand ecological processes that influence this LaMP restoration goal. Thus, there is a need to consider the primary drivers within the ecosystem that affect fish contamination and provide direction for restoration efforts. We used the framework to address this need; the following discussions are drawn from the example table, appendix 1.

Geomorphic Processes

Geomorphic processes that affect the "We can all eat the fish" LaMP goal relate to distribution and retention of contaminants in the ecosystem. Important processes include the adherence of contaminants to substrate and the leaching of legacy contaminants that regulate bioavailability, as well the determination of watershed shape by landscape contours, which influences the distribution of depositional areas, shoreline energy, and shoreline erosion. Adherence to substrate is important because contaminants that are dissolved or weakly bound to substrate are more bioavailable than structurally complex contaminants. Retention and the subsequent dissolution of legacy contaminants from substrate into the water (leaching) is an important process because in high-energy coastal zones or large watersheds, contaminant transport tends to be dominated by surface runoff, current upwellings and downwellings, and nearshore currents; in low-energy areas, by contrast, bed sediments are the major route of contaminant exposure to organisms (Burton and Johnston, 2010). Thus, sediment attributes and landscape attributes create spatial variability in contaminants within Lake Michigan. Fine-scale processes of sediment transport and deposition regulate contact between sediment and contaminants, because suspended sediments provide large amounts of surface area for contaminant adsorption. The sizes of deposited sediment particles that make up the lake substrate influence the availability of the sediment pore space for transporting contaminants and subsequent contaminant exposure to bottom-dwelling animal species through ingestion or direct adsorption. MacDonald and others (2000) reported that PCBs were highly toxic to sediment-dwelling organisms, a finding that has implications for exposure and bioaccumulation for other animals that consume them. Contaminants within sediments in the coastal/ nearshore and watershed zones can be transferred to terrestrial species via food-web connections. For example, Raikow and others (2011) reported that lake-origin PCBs were detected up to 30 m inland in wasps. In that study, PCBs originated from contaminated emergent aquatic invertebrates inhabiting contaminated lake sediments that wasps consumed. The role of sediment contaminants is critical to the need for FCAs, but the fate of contaminants in both disturbed sediments and sediments that are subject to major disturbances is not well understood (Eggleton and Thomas, 2004).

Anthropogenic modifications such as the construction of shoreline stabilization structures—or "shoreline hardening" —and dredging can alter geomorphic processes that determine contaminant retention and thus affect transport processes among lake zones. For example, channel construction can convert areas of sediment deposition to higher-flow, nondepositional areas and thus disturb historically settled contaminants and change distribution patterns of contaminants. Although anthropogenic modifications are of greater concern within the coastal/nearshore and watershed zones than in the open-lake zone, sites for disposing of dredging spoil are sometimes situated in the open-lake zone, and dredging-spoil disposal could potentially distribute contaminants that originated inshore to the open-lake zone. Riverbank alterations can also create opportunities for the movement of contaminants from recognizable "point" locations during rewetting events if contaminated sediments have been placed within erosional areas of the watershed (Burton and Johnston, 2010). The use and security of confined disposal facilities determine the risk of recontamination.

Hydrologic Processes

Hydrologic processes also influence the loading and transport of contaminants within the Lake Michigan ecosystem. The manufacturing of many contaminants that are harmful to fish has been banned for decades—for example, PCBs were banned in the United States in 1979. Yet, there are legacy sources for most banned contaminants, and some contaminants are still actively produced—for example, mercury emissions from coal-fired power plants. Carlson and others (2010) reported that the major source for most contaminants within the Great Lakes is airborne deposition—a "nonpoint" source that cannot be traced to a single source—and the major contaminant deposition areas are sediments. Single, identifiable sources of contaminants (point sources) are now negligible sources of contaminants within the Great Lakes region (Carlson and others, 2010). Airborne deposition is the largest source of many contaminants, and mercury concentrations in fish are related to localized atmospheric concentrations across much of the United States (Hammerschmidt and Fitzgerald, 2006). Multiple models have been developed to explore atmospheric deposition and the exchange of contaminants, such as PCBs, between the atmosphere and the water surface (Meng and others, 2008); however, future dynamics and contaminant loadings are difficult to predict. In contrast, sources of CECs have been traced to agricultural, municipal, industrial, and sewage wastes (Lee and others, 2012), thus creating opportunities to link hydrological processes to CEC contaminant loadings.

The hydrologic transport of contaminants across and within ecosystem zones is complex and would benefit from additional research. Specific transport properties vary depending on individual contaminants and hydrologic setting in the Great Lakes. Within the open-lake zone, lake-water mixing and large-scale circulation patterns likely drive the deposition of contaminants. For example, fall turnover of different layers of water in Lake Superior could resuspend PCBs from sediment into the water column and increase their net residence time (Baker and others, 1985). Finer scale dynamics such as the deposition of contaminants in sediment, their burial, and then their localized resuspension have been modeled; one example is a mass-balance PCB model for Lake Ontario by Mackay (1989). Within the nearshore zone, contaminant loading is affected by surrounding landscape uses. For example, the Atmospheric Exchange Over Lakes and Oceans project hypothesized that increased urban emissions of hazardous air pollutants resulted in increased atmospheric depositional fluxes to adjacent Great Lakes waters (Simcik and others, 1999), and an "urban plume" of PCB-enriched precipitation affecting Lake Michigan that stemmed from Chicago has been documented (Offenberg and Baker, 1997). Within the coastal/nearshore zone, longshore currents—as well as episodic events such as upwellings, storm-induced surges, and spring runoff—act to distribute contaminants and disturb sediments, thereby resulting in contaminant resuspension in water.

Studies of sediment trapping have measured contaminant settling and resuspension across a range of time scales, but we are not aware that anyone has related these measures to the bioavailability of contaminants. Contaminant loading and dispersion within the watershed is influenced by local population sizes, hydrologic flows, and flow seasonality.

Anthropogenic influences can exacerbate hydrological processes affecting loading and distribution of contaminants. Of greatest concern are human activities that magnify airborne deposition. Within the coastal/nearshore and watershed zones, both point and nonpoint loadings create concerns for contaminant loading. For example, Whittle and Fitzsimmons (1983) concluded that the Niagara River was a major source of contaminants and trace metals to Lake Ontario. Although point sources in the watershed have been greatly reduced via water-quality policies, infrequent accidents can result in punctuated loadings with long-term implications.

Biological Processes

Biological processes determine the transfer of contaminants into fish tissue. Given the bioaccumulative nature of most fish contaminants of concern in Lake Michigan, the need for FCAs is dependent on species-specific characteristics including the predator's level in the food web, also referred to as "trophic level"; its primary prey type; its gross growth efficiency (that is, the proportion of food it consumes that goes towards growth); and its contaminant retention efficiency, meaning the proportion of contaminants it consumes that it does not excrete (Madenjian, Schmidt, and others 1999). For example, lake trout have 80-percent total PCB retention efficiency, whereas Coho salmon have 50-percent total PCB retention efficiency, although both fish species have very similar alewife-dependent diets (Madenjian, Schmidt, and others, 1999). Variations in the accumulation of contaminants within the same fish species can be explained by differences in gender, age, size, food-consumption rates, growth rates, and activity rates (Trudel and Rasmussen, 2006; Madenjian and others, 2010, 2011). Also important are contaminant concentrations in prey and contaminant toxicity (for example, PCB congener variability).

The biological processes we identified that influence contaminant transfer through the food web are the same in all zones; however, the contributing components in each zone may differ. This difference is largely due to variations in biogeochemical activity, biological communities, and predator-prey interactions within the watershed, coastal/nearshore, and open-lake zones. Food-web linkages across these zones are not well understood.

Anthropogenic influences can exacerbate processes that limit meeting the LaMP restoration goal of safe fish consumption. Introductions of low and middle trophic level invasive species can lengthen food chains, decrease energy transfer, and cause increased consumption needs for native top predators; thus potentially magnifying bioaccumulation of contaminants. Introductions of prey species can also shift predator diet

compositions (for example, lake trout now commonly feed on benthic, invasive, round goby *Neogobius melanostomus*) causing the risk of contaminant exposure from eating any particular species to change through time. Human influences on climate can result in changes in exchange rates between atmospheric sources and water, as well as increases in the production rates of lower trophic level fish, and these changes would affect contaminant delivery to sediments and contaminant accumulation in predatory fish. Lastly, temperature changes would affect fish metabolic parameters, thus increasing predator feeding rates and potentially affecting contaminant elimination rates.

What We Know from Monitoring Efforts

Extensive diet analysis and bioenergetics modeling have provided much insight into Lake Michigan food-web processes influencing FCAs. Several intensive sampling opportunities every 5–10 years, such as the Lake Michigan Mass Balance Study, the Great Lakes Cooperative Science and Monitoring Initiative, and the Great Lakes Restoration Initiative, have provided support for investigating predator-prey interactions, food-web connections, and bioenergetics-based exploration of bioaccumulation within multiple fishery target species (for example, McCarty and others, 2004; Davis and others, 2007).

Studies of individual physical and chemical properties of contaminants create generalized expectations of contaminant half-lives and their behaviors within aquatic systems. Variations in contaminant physical and chemical properties within Lake Michigan should be expected given the range of energy, sediment, and transport processes across the ecosystem.

Examples of Knowledge Gaps

Two examples of knowledge gaps that limit the ability to prioritize restoration actions for achieving the LaMP goal "We can all eat the fish" are provided below. The first shows that the process of contaminant loading to fish is understood, but data gaps limit our understanding of fish contaminant burdens in Lake Michigan. The second example illustrates a case where processes affecting circulation of contaminants and dispersal linkages among Lake Michigan zones are not well understood.

Because trophic-level influence on fish contaminant loads is well understood, increased monitoring could inform how spatial and temporal variability in fish diets affect contaminant burdens in their tissues. To further complicate the issue, recent evidence suggests that the contaminant burden of a prey fish can vary in response to changes in its diet. Altogether, these data gaps suggest that more regular monitoring of the diets of predatory fish under FCAs, as well as the diets and contaminant burdens of their primary prey, would help us better understand the primary sources of variation in contaminant loads for fishes under FCAs. Spatial variability in contaminant burdens is best exemplified by the finding that male walleye (*Sander vitreus*) had higher PCB concentrations than females in the Saginaw River system, because males spent more time in upstream areas where prey fish had high contaminant concentrations (Madenjian and others, 1998). Temporal variability in contaminant burdens of Chinook salmon would be detected by existing monitoring, but our understanding of this variation is limited. For example, Lake Michigan Chinook salmon diets consist of more than 75 percent alewife, and adult alewife had exponentially decreasing PCB loads from 4.5 milligrams per kilogram (mg/kg) in 1976 to 1.0 mg/kg in 1985 (Madenjian and others, 1993); PCB loads in alewife further declined to less than 0.5 mg/kg by 1994–95 (Madenjian and others, 1999). Declining alewife PCB concentrations coincided with declining alewife energy density, and thus total consumption of alewife had to increase to sustain the growth rates of their predators. How these changes influenced PCB loads of Chinook salmon over this same time period is unclear. Furthermore, recent species invasions have resulted in uncoupling of the Lake Michigan food web, resulting in fish diet changes that could influence the fishes' contaminant burdens. For example, dreissenid mussels have recently become larger components of lake whitefish diets (Pothoven and Madenjian 2008), but how this diet shift has influenced lake whitefish contaminant burden or contaminant retention has not been evaluated. Regular monitoring of prey-fish contaminant burdens—for example, monitoring every 2 years—along with regular evaluation of predator diet composition and investigations of food-web linkages would improve our understanding of trends in contaminant burdens in Lake Michigan fish and our ability to achieve this LaMP goal.

Dispersal processes that result in contaminant loadings within and across lake zones, such as those between the coastal/nearshore and offshore zones, are not well understood. Although we have identified plausibly important influences that are largely associated with hydrologic processes, we cannot identify the relative importance of these influences to contaminant dispersal. Biological processes also influence contaminant circulation; for example, riverine fish and invertebrates can become contaminated after eating the eggs of nonnative Pacific salmon species that reside for most of their lives within the open lake and return to Great Lakes tributaries to spawn (Merna, 1986). Evidence exists that contaminant concentrations in a Lake Ontario tributary increased in response to the death and decay of Chinook salmon after their spawning runs (O'Toole and others, 2006). Thus, fish behaviors can influence contaminant dispersal across zones, but their importance relative to hydrologic processes is not well understood. On a lakewide scale, we are not aware of knowledge that provides explicit, process-based linkages between localized contaminant hot spots" and resultant fish contaminant loads. Understanding processes that drive contaminant dispersal and within-lake sources would provide direction for restoration efforts.

References

Baker, J.E., Eisenreich, S.J., Johnson, T.C., and Halfman, B.M., 1985, Chlorinated hydrocarbon cycling in the benthic nepheloid layer of Lake Superior: Environmental Science and Technology, v. 19, p. 853–861.

Burton, G.A., and Johnston, E.L., 2010, Assessing contaminated sediments in the context of multiple stressors: Environmental Toxicology and Chemistry, v. 29, no. 12, p. 2625–2643.

Carlson, D.L., De Vault, D.S., and Swackhammer, D.L., 2010, On the rate of decline of persistent organic contaminants in lake trout (*Salvelinus namaycush*) from the Great Lakes, 1970–2003: Environmental Science and Technology, v. 44, no. 6, p. 2004–2010.

Davis, B.M., Savino, J.F., and Ogilvie, L.M., 2007, Diet niches of major forage fish in Lake Michigan: Advances in Limnology, v. 60, p. 261–275.

Eggleton, J., and Thomas, K.V., 2004, A review of factors affecting the release and bioavailability of contaminants during sediment disturbance events: Environment International, v. 30, p. 973–980.

Food and Agriculture Organization of the United Nations, 2010, Fishery and aquaculture statistics, 2008: Yearbook no. 932, 72 p.

Gebhardt, S.E., and Thomas, R.G., 2002, Nutritive value of foods: U.S. Department of Agriculture, Agricultural Research Service, Home and Garden Bulletin 72, 95 p., accessed April 17, 2013, at *http://www.nal.usda.gov/fnic/foodcomp/Data/HG72/hg72_2002.pdf*.

Goyer, R.A., Aposhian, H.V., Arab, L., Bellinger, D.C., Burbacher, T.M., Burke, T.A., Jacobson, J.L., Knobeloch, L.M., Ryan, L.M., and Stern, A.H., 2000, Toxological Effects of Methylmercury, National Academy Press, Washington, D.C., 344 p.

Hammerschmidt, C.R., and Fitzgerald, W.F., 2006, Methylmercury in freshwater fish linked to atmospheric mercury deposition: Environmental Science and Technology, v. 40, no. 24, p. 7764–7770.

Jeremiason, J.D., Eisenreich, S.J., Baker, J.E., and Eadie, B.J., 1998, PCB decline in settling particles and benthic recycling of PCBs and PAHs in Lake Superior: Environmental Science and Technology, v. 32, p. 3249–3256.

Lee, K.E., Langer, S.K., Menheer, M.A., Foreman, W.T., Furlong, E.T., and Smith, S.G., 2012, Chemicals of emerging concern in water and bottom sediment in Great Lakes areas of concern, 2010–2011—Collection methods, analyses, methods, quality assurance, and data: U.S. Geological Survey Data Series 723, 26 p.

MacDonald D., DiPinto, L.M., Field, J., Ingersoll, C.G., Long, E.R., and Swartz, R.C., 2000, Development and evaluation of consensus-based sediment effect concentration for polychlorinated biphenyls: Environmental Toxicology and Chemistry, v. 19, no. 5, p. 1403–1413.

Mackay, D., 1989, Modeling the long-term behavior of an organic contaminant in a large lake—Application to PCBs in Lake Ontario: Journal of Great Lakes Research, v. 15, no. 2, p. 283–297.

Madenjian, C.P., Carpenter, S.R., Eck, G.W., and Miller, M.A., 1993, Accumulation of PCBs by lake trout (*Salvelinus namaycush*)—An individual-based model approach: Canadian Journal of Fisheries and Aquatic Sciences, v. 50, no. 1, p. 97–109.

Madenjian, C.P., DeSorcie, T.J., Stedman, R.M., Brown, E.H., Jr., Eck, G.W., Schmidt, L.J., Hesselberg, R.J., Chernyak, S.M., and Passino-Reader, D.R., 1999, Spatial patterns in PCB concentrations of Lake Michigan lake trout: Journal of Great Lakes Research, v. 25, no. 1, p. 149–159.

Madenjian, C.P., Keir, M.J., and Whittle, D.M., 2011, Sexual difference in mercury concentrations of lake trout (*Salvelinus namaycush*) from Lake Ontario: Chemosphere, v. 83, p. 903–908.

Madenjian, C.P., Keir, M.J., Whittle, D.M., and Noguchi, G.E., 2010, Sexual difference in PCB concentrations of lake trout (*Salvelinus namaycush*) from Lake Ontario: Science of the Total Environment, v. 408, p. 1725–1730.

Madenjian, C.P., Noguchi, G.E., Hass, R.C., and Schrouder, K.S., 1998, Sexual difference in polychlorinated biphenyl accumulation rates of walleye (*Stizostedion vitreum*): Canadian Journal of Fisheries and Aquatic Sciences, v. 55, p. 1085–1092.

Madenjian, C.P., Schmidt, L.J., Chernyak, S.M., Elliott, R.F., DeSorcie, T.J., Quintal, R.T., Begnoche, L.J., and Hesselberg, R.J., 1999, Variation in net trophic transfer efficiencies among 21 PCB congeners: Environmental Science and Technology, v. 33, p. 3768–3773.

McCarty, H.B., Schofield, J., Miller, K., Brent, R.N., Van Hoof, P., and Eadie, B., 2004. Results of the Lake Michigan Mass Balance Study—Polychlorinated biphenyls and *trans*-nonachlor data report: U.S. Environmental Protection Agency, Great Lakes National Program Office, EPA 905–R–01–011 [variously paged].

Meng, F., Wen, D., and Sloan, J., 2008, Modelling of air-water exchange of PCBs in the Great Lakes: Atmospheric Environment, v. 42, p. 4822–4835.

Merna, J.W., 1986, Contamination of stream fishes with chlorinated hydrocarbons from eggs of Great Lakes salmon: Transactions of the American Fisheries Society, v. 115, p. 69–74.

Mozaffarian, D., and Rimm, E.B., 2006, Fish intake, contaminants, and human health—Evaluating the risks and benefits: Journal of the American Medical Association, v. 296, no. 15, p. 1885–1899.

Offenberg, J.H., and Baker, J.E., 1997, Polychlorinated biphenyls in Chicago precipitation—Enhanced wet deposition to near-shore Lake Michigan: Environmental Science and Technology, v. 31, p. 1534–1538.

O'Toole, S., Metcalfe, C., Craine, I., and Gross, M., 2006, Release of persistent organic contaminants from carcasses of Lake Ontario Chinook salmon (*Oncorhynchus tshawytscha*): Environmental Pollution, v. 140, p. 102–113.

Pothoven, S.A., and Madenjian, C.P., 2008, Changes in consumption by alewives and lake whitefish after dreissenid mussel invasions in Lakes Michigan and Huron: North American Journal of Fisheries Management, v. 28, p. 308–320.

Raikow, D.F., Walters, D.M., Fritz, K.M., and Mills, M.A., 2011, The distance that contaminated aquatic subsidies extend into lake riparian zones: Ecological Applications, v. 21, no. 3, p. 983–990.

Sidhu, K.S., 2003, Health benefits and potential risks related to consumption of fish or fish oil: Regulatory Toxicology and Pharmacology, v. 38, no. 3, p. 336–344.

Simcik, M.F., Eisenreich, S.J., and Lioy, P.J., 1999, Source apportionment and source/sink relationships of PAHs in the coastal atmosphere of Chicago and Lake Michigan: Atmospheric Environment, v. 33, p. 5071–5079.

U.S. Environmental Protection Agency and Environment Canada, 2009, Nearshore areas of the Great Lakes 2009: State of the Great Lakes 2009 Reports, EPA 905–R–09–013, p. 108–112.

Trudel, M., and Rasmussen, J.B., 2006, Bioenergetics and mercury dynamics in fish—A modelling perspective: Canadian Journal of Fisheries and Aquatic Sciences, v. 63, p. 1890–1902.

Welcomme, R.L., Cowx, I.G., Coates, D., Béné, C., Funge-Smith, S., Halls, A., and Lorenzen, K., 2010, Inland capture fisheries: Philosophical Transactions of the Royal Society B, v. 365, p. 2881–2896.

Whittle, D.M., and Fitzsimons, J.D., 1983, The influence of the Niagara River on contaminant burdens of Lake Ontario biota: Journal of Great Lakes Research, v. 9, no. 2, p. 295–302.

Chicago Lakefront, Daniel Schwen ©①③

We Can All Drink the Water

Importance of Drinking Water to Lake Michigan Communities

Safe drinking water is of critical importance to Lake Michigan communities. Drinking water is taken from public-water-supply intakes tapping the nearshore zone, groundwater, or rivers or other surface water within the Lake Michigan basin. There are 31 direct Lake Michigan drinking-water intakes in Illinois, 25 in Wisconsin, 22 in Michigan, and 7 in Indiana. Water use for each Great Lakes basin has recently been compiled through 2005 (Mills and Sharpe, 2010), and the Lake Michigan basin accounted for 15 billion gallons per day (Bgal/day)—an estimated 12.3 Bgal/day was taken directly from Lake Michigan. This was 49 percent of all U.S. water withdrawn from the Great Lakes region, but much of this water was for uses other than public water supply, such as thermoelectric power or use. Within the Lake Michigan Basin, 1.5 Bgal/day from surface water was used for public water supply; from groundwater, 295 million gallons per day (Mgal/day) was used for public water supply, and 178 Mgal/day was used for private (domestic) water supply, all sources together serving a population of about 7.7 million people. There are few estimates of the economic values associated with clean drinking water; however, the *Cryptosporidium* outbreak in Milwaukee, Wis., in 1993 was estimated to cost $96.2 million: $31.7 million in medical costs and $64.6 million in productivity loss (Corso and others, 2003). Austin and others (2007) estimated that operating costs for water-supply facilities using Great Lakes water totaled about $600 million in 2006 dollars and that the Great lakes Regional Collaboration goal of achieving a 40-percent reduction in sedimentation might reduce drinking-water treatment costs by $12 million annually. Many industries also rely on high-quality water for their processes.

Drinking-Water Monitoring

The U.S. Environmental Protection Agency (EPA) Office of Groundwater and Drinking Water has the primary role of ensuring that drinking water from public water supplies is protected. The EPA does not typically regulate private water supplies. In the States of the Lake Michigan basin, various agencies at several levels of government may require some tests of water quality when private water supplies are installed or when property is sold. These tests are rarely as extensive as those required by the EPA for public water supplies. The EPA has established National Primary Drinking Water Regulations, which are legally enforceable standards for public water systems. The EPA also maintains a database, the Safe Drinking Water Information System at *http://water.epa.gov/scitech/datait/databases/drink/sdwisfed/index.cfm*, listing monitoring results and monitoring and standards violations for public water supplies (U.S. Environmental Protection Agency, 2012a). The EPA requires public water systems to be monitored for selected microbiological, inorganic, organic, and radiological contaminants listed at *http://water.epa.gov/drink/contaminants/index.cfm#1.* (U.S. Environmental Protection Agency, 2012b). Further, the EPA requires each community water system to generate an annual Consumer Confidence Report (*http://cfpub.epa.gov/safewater/ccr/*; U.S. Environmental Protection Agency, 2012c) that is made available to all residents receiving water from that water system. Summary reports by year and state can be obtained at *http://water.epa.gov/scitech/datait/databases/drink/sdwisfed/*.

The contaminants required by the EPA to be monitored in public water supplies are typically those that have been identified to be of concern in source water for drinking-water supplies. Among these are many contaminants that are of general concern in the Lake Michigan Basin, such as industrial contaminants and persistent organic chemicals, or the protozoan *Cryptosporidium*, which caused the largest drinking water-related outbreak of illness in U.S. history in Milwaukee, Wis., in 1993. In addition, some inorganic contaminants such as mercury and arsenic, which may have natural sources, or nitrate, which is often associated with excess fertilizer use or septic-system contamination of groundwater, are also required to be monitored in public water supplies. The Safe Drinking Water Act includes a process that the EPA must follow to identify and list unregulated contaminants that may require a national drinking-water regulation in the future. The EPA must periodically publish a Contaminant Candidate List (CCL; *http://water.epa.gov/scitech/drinkingwater/dws/ccl/index.cfm*; U.S. Environmental Protection Agency, 2012d) and decide whether or not to regulate at least five or more contaminants on the list. The newest CCL (CCL3) lists several endocrine-disrupting compounds such as hormones or hormone-like substances, and their addition to the CCL may have resulted from recent findings of pharmaceutical and personal care products in the Nation's drinking-water supplies (Snyder and others, 2008).

The Waterborne Disease and Outbreak Surveillance System is a national surveillance system maintained by the U.S. Centers for Disease Control and Prevention. This system receives data about waterborne disease outbreaks and summarizes and publishes the data. The most recent summary (for 2005–6; Centers for Disease Control and Prevention, 2008) can be found at *http://www.cdc.gov/mmwr/pdf/ss/ss5709.pdf*. This summary notes a trend of increasing outbreaks caused by *Legionella* bacteria and also by contaminated groundwater.

Most States completed Source Water Assessments for their public drinking-water supplies in the early 2000s (*http://water.epa.gov/infrastructure/drinkingwater/sourcewater/protection/sourcewaterassessments.cfm*; U.S. Environmental Protection Agency, 2012e). Each assessment report defined a delineated protection area, identified an inventory of potential sources of contamination, and conducted an evaluation of the likelihood of the water system being contaminated.

Identifying Key Processes and Uncertainties

Current monitoring programs for drinking water are focused on *public* water supplies and on specific contaminants *previously* found to cause adverse health effects from drinking water. The EPA's list of National Primary Drinking Water contaminants identifies the suspected sources for most of those constituents. Nevertheless, the sources of many contaminants are located at some distance from the drinking-water intake or well or are diffusely distributed across the landscape. For recently recognized contaminants, such as many microorganisms and constituents on the CCL, the sources and pathways to the drinking-water intake or well may be unknown. For many microbiological contaminants, the processes that govern their survival or persistence in the environment are poorly known. We used the framework to address this need; the following discussions are drawn from the example table, appendix 2.

Geomorphic Processes

The natural geology of an area surrounding a drinking-water intake or well may influence the water quality of that water supply. For example, arsenic is a naturally occurring inorganic compound that has caused unacceptable quality of groundwater in parts of southeastern Michigan (*http://www.michigan.gov/documents/arsenicbroch_41426_7.pdf*; Michigan Department of Community Health and Michigan Department of Environmental Quality, 2006) and Wisconsin (*http://dnr.wi.gov/topic/Groundwater/arsenic/index.html*; Wisconsin Department of Natural Resources, no date). In addition, the natural geology may facilitate contamination of groundwater from surface sources. Porous or fractured limestone (karst) occurs on the western side of Lake Michigan and extends through the Door Peninsula and onto the Garden Peninsula in Michigan; this material is especially susceptible to contamination from surface sources such as agriculture, industry, or leaking septic systems (*http://wi.water.usgs.gov/gwcomp/find/door/susceptibility.html*; University of Wisconsin Extension and U.S. Geological Survey, 2007) and will be an important concern for groundwater supplies both public and private (homeowner wells). Likewise, the vulnerability of shallow groundwater supplies—public or private—to nitrate contamination from agricultural fertilizer application has been evaluated (Chowdhury and others, 2003; Saad, 2008), and it again is a function of local geologic materials. For drinking-water intakes that extend into Lake Michigan, geomorphic factors within the lake may be important. For example, currents and locations where sediments accumulate may influence the susceptibility of drinking-water intakes to contamination.

Hydrologic Processes

Hydrologic processes that influence nearshore drinking-water intakes include flow and transport from watersheds or storm drains, nearshore groundwater, longshore currents, interaction between nearshore and large lake currents, waves, and the effects of each of these on nearshore sediments or sands. Rao and Schwab (2007) reviewed hydrologic interactions between the open Great Lakes, the coastal boundary layer, and the surf and swash zones. They pointed out that we are "…still a long way from having predictive understanding of the dynamics of sediment, contaminant, and pathogen transport near beaches," and this statement would also apply to the zone where drinking-water intakes are located. All of these complex hydrologic factors may be operational; however, the significance of each factor may vary from day to day. The final draft "Source Water Assessment Report for the City of South Haven, Mich." noted a probable influence of the plume of water from the Black River when the wind direction was from the north-northeast and was sustained for 24 to 36 hours (U.S. Geological Survey and Michigan Department of Environmental Quality, 2003, at *http://www.south-haven.com/pages/public_works/pdf/Source-Water-Assessment-Report.pdf*). In addition, the amount of solid particles suspended in water (turbidity) was recorded to increase when wind was from the south through southwest; the increase was likely due to currents and sediment resuspension in Lake Michigan. Just this one example shows the importance of hydrology in Lake Michigan and in nearby rivers to a single drinking-water system.

Public water supplies that draw from groundwater also are influenced by hydrologic characteristics, such as ground-water traveltimes and direction, which in turn influence the potential delivery of contaminants from surface or under-ground sources to their wells. Private drinking-water wells are similarly susceptible to surface or underground hydrologic transport processes, but they are rarely assessed. Finally, drinking water drawn from rivers is particularly susceptible to the hydrologic features of those rivers and the distance and traveltime to the intake from contaminant sources such as wastewater treatment plants, industrial outfalls, or agricultural wastes.

Biological Processes

The vast majority of drinking-water-related outbreaks of disease or illness are caused by biological agents (Craun and others, 2006). For the period 1991–2002, 16 percent of outbreaks were due to chemical poisoning. (During 1971–90, only 10 percent were due to chemical poisoning.) The rest were caused by a variety of bacteria or viruses, although the "unidentified" cause category was the largest in both report-ing periods, causing 38–52 percent of illness outbreaks. It is widely assumed that the true incidence of waterborne disease is underreported (Craun and others, 2006; Reynolds and others, 2008); 19.5 million cases of waterborne disease per year nationwide have been estimated (Reynolds and others, 2008).

The most frequently identified agents between 1991 and 2002 were *Cryptosporidium* and *Giardia* protozoa. Ingestion of only a small number of these organisms can cause infection. They can survive not only long periods in cold water but also many types of water treatment, and their presence is not specifically indicated by tests for fecal indicator bacteria (FIB) such as fecal coliform bacteria or *Escherichia coli*—the most commonly used indicators of microbiological pollution. Like-wise, viruses have many of the same survival characteristics as protozoa, but methods to analyze water for them are so dif-ficult and costly that their prevalence is likely underestimated. Viruses such as reoviruses, enteroviruses, and adenovirusues have been detected in wastewater-treatment-plant influent and effluent in Milwaukee, Wis. (Sedmak and others, 2005). Additionally, 18 of 204 Lake Michigan source water samples for the Milwaukee drinking-water plant tested positive for reoviruses. Pediatric emergency diarrheal illness increased after release of undertreated sewage in Milwaukee, Wis. (Redman and others, 2007), and in two of six cases where undertreated sewage was released, there was a statistically significant increase in the number of hospital visits by people living in Lake Michigan ZIP codes. Septic-system density is

associated with household infectious diarrhea for children less than 19 years old in households on private well-water supply in Wisconsin, according to a study by Borchardt and others (2003). This study and an additional study of groundwater and river-water supplies in Wisconsin showed no relation between the detection of viruses and the numbers of FIB (Borchardt and others, 2003, 2004). These few studies demonstrate that much more needs to be learned about the actual pathogens causing waterborne disease in the Lake Michigan Basin.

In addition, taste and odor problems are a challenge for drinking-water systems, especially those that use surface water. If the taste and odor problem is an earthy or fishy smell, it may be due to the growth of cyanobacteria (sometimes called blue-green algae) that release odor-causing compounds. Large growths of cyanobacteria may also release more problematic compounds—toxins that affect the nervous system or liver function—and such a growth may be referred to as a "harmful algal bloom" (HAB). A recent study (Graham and others, 2010) showed that in samples collected from 23 Midwestern lakes, taste- and odor-producing compounds co-occurred with microcystin (a cyanotoxin) in 91 percent of algal blooms. It is clear that blooms of cyanobacteria do occur in the Great Lakes (*http://www.glerl.noaa.gov/res/Centers/HABS/index.html;* National Oceanic and Atmospheric Administration, no date), but little is known about their origins and distributions or about the toxins released (Dyble and others, 2008). The National Oceanic and Atmospheric Administration (NOAA) Great Lakes Environmental Research Center has developed an experimental HAB forecast bulletin for Lake Erie, where HABs have become problematic (*http://www.glerl.noaa.gov/ res/Centers/HABS/lake_erie_hab/lake_erie_hab.html;* National Oceanic and Atmospheric Administration, 2012). This forecast system relies on an understanding of the biological factors that influence cyanobacteria growth and the hydrologic factors that allow blooms to concentrate. A recent study by the EPA (2009) recorded low levels of microcystin, one of the most common toxins produced by cyanobacteria, in many inland lakes of the Lake Michigan Basin. Still, there is no standard for microcys-tin in drinking water or recreational water in the United States; the World Health Organization (1998) recommends a con-centration less than 1 microgram per liter of microcystin-LR (a particular form of microcystin) in drinking water.

What We Know from Monitoring Efforts

From existing monitoring programs there is much infor-mation about the range of contaminants affecting public water supplies and about specific contaminants for which health effects have previously been determined. Each public water utility has completed a Source Water Assessment that identi-fied many of the major potential threats to that supply. Data are widely disseminated for required contaminant monitoring, and most water supplies provide very good water as measured by current standards and constituents. Little is known about con-taminants in private water supplies, and little is known about chemicals of emerging concern (CECs).

Knowledge Gaps and Uncertainties

One key uncertainty is the lack of epidemiological or analytic data for most pathogens that may be found in most water supplies, public or private. Substantial information is available about the causes and sources of outbreaks of contaminants in drinking water that are sufficiently large to attract attention; however, it is widely understood that the human disease burden due to contaminated drinking water is underestimated or not captured by current monitoring or outbreak-related data. Little is known about the influence of HABs in Lake Michigan on public health, there are no standards for cyanobacterial toxins in drinking water, and there is no monitoring program for HABs or for their toxins.

Very little is known about the geomorphic, hydrologic, or biological factors that influence the concentration, transport, and health risk of recently recognized contaminants. In some cases, these contaminants may derive from sources not considered in Source Water Assessments. For example, chloride concentrations have been increasing over the past several decades in groundwater and surface water in and around the Lake Michigan Basin (Mullaney and others, 2009) and in the Great Lakes themselves (*http://www.epa.gov/greatlakes/monitoring/limnology/index.html*); the assumed sources for chloride are road salt from stormwater runoff, wastewater or septic-system contamination, or agricultural practices. All these sources contain numerous CECs, but there has been little study of whether the increase in chloride concentrations may signal an associated increase in CECs in Great Lakes drinking-water supplies. There is little monitoring for recently recognized contaminants, and only a few focused studies addressing drinking water in the Lake Michigan Basin.

References

Austin, J.C., Anderson, S., Courant, P.N., and Litan, R.E., 2007, America's North Coast—A benefit-cost analysis of a program to protect and restore the Great Lakes, accessed April 17, 2013, at *http://www.healthylakes.org/site_upload/upload/America_s_North_Coast_Report_07.pdf*.

Borchardt, M.A., Haas, N.L., and Hunt, R. J., 2004, Vulnerability of drinking-water wells in La Crosse, Wisconsin, to enteric-virus contamination from surface water contributions: Applied and Environmental Microbiology, v. 70, p. 5937–5946.

Borchardt, M.A., Bertz, P.D., Spencer, S.K., and Battigelli, D.A., 2003, Incidence of enteric viruses in groundwater from household wells in Wisconsin: Applied and Environmental Microbiology, v. 69, p. 1172–1180.

Centers for Disease Control and Prevention, 2008, Surveillance summaries: Morbidity and Mortality Weekly Report, v. 57, no SS–9, 72 p., accessed June 22, 2012, at *http://www.cdc.gov/mmwr/pdf/ss/ss5709.pdf*.

Chowdhury, S.H., Kehew, A.E., and Passero, R.N., 2003, Correlation between nitrate contamination and ground water pollution potential: Ground Water, v. 41, p. 735–745.

Corso, P.S., Kramer, M.H., Blair, K.A., Addiss, D.G., Davis, J.P., and Haddix, A.C., 2003, Cost of illness in the 1993 waterborne *Cryptosporidium* outbreak, Milwaukee, Wisconsin: Emerging Infectious Disease, v. 9, p. 426–431.

Craun, M.F., Craun, G.F., Calderon, R.L., and Beach, M.J., 2006, Waterborne outbreaks reported in the United States: Journal of Water and Health, v. 4, supp. 2, p. 19–30.

Dyble, J., Bienfang, P., Dusek, E., Hitchcock, G., Holland, F., Laws, E., Lerczak, J., McGillicuddy, D.J., Jr., Minnet, P., Moore, S.K., O'Kelly, C., Solo-Gabriel, H., and Wang, J.D., 2008, Environmental controls, oceanography, and population dynamics of pathogens and harmful algal blooms—Connecting sources to human exposure: Environmental Health, v. 7, supp. 2, article S5, 13 p.

Graham, J.L., Loftin, K.A., Meyer, M.T., and Ziegler, A.C., 2010, Cyanotoxin mixtures and taste-and-odor compounds in cyanobacterial blooms from the Midwestern United States: Environmental Science and Technology, v. 44, no. 19, p. 7361–7368, *http://dx.doi.org/doi:10.1021/es1008938*.

Michigan Department of Community Health and Michigan Department of Environmental Quality, 2006, Arsenic in well water, health information for well users: Michigan Department of Environmental Quality, 2 p., accessed June 21, 2012, at *http://www.michigan.gov/documents/arsenicbroch_41426_7.pdf*.

Mills, P.C., and Sharpe, J.B., 2010, Estimated withdrawals and other elements of water use in the Great Lakes Basin of the United States in 2005: U.S. Geological Survey Scientific Investigations Report 2010–5031, 95 p., available online at *http://pubs.usgs.gov/sir/2010/5031/*.

Mullaney, J.R., Lorenz, D.L., and Arntson, A.D., 2009, Chloride in groundwater and surface water in areas underlain by the glacial aquifer system, northern United States: U.S. Geological Survey Scientific Investigations Report 2009–5086, 41 p., available online at *http://pubs.usgs.gov/sir/2009/5086/*.

National Oceanic and Atmospheric Administration [n.d.], Harmful algal blooms data & products: Center of Excellence for Great Lakes Human Health, accessed June 21, 2012, at *http://www.glerl.noaa.gov/res/Centers/HABS/index.html*.

National Oceanic and Atmospheric Administration, 2012, Supplemental information on experimental Lake Erie Harmful Algal Bloom bulletin: Great Lakes Environmental Research Laboratory, Bulletin 0, 2 p., accessed June 21, 2012, at *http://www.glerl.noaa.gov/res/Centers/HABS/lake_erie_hab/bulletin_2012-000.pdf*.

Rao, Y.R., and Schwab, D.J., 2007, Transport and mixing between the coastal and offshore waters in the Great Lakes—A review: Journal of Great Lakes Research, v. 33, p. 202–218.

Redman, R., Nenn, C., Eastwood, D., and Gorelick, M., 2007, Pediatric emergency department visits for diarrheal illness increased after release of untreated sewage: Pediatrics, v. 120, no. 6, p. 1472–1475.

Reynolds, K.A., Mena, K.D., and Gerba, C.P., 2008, Risk of waterborne illness via drinking water in the United States: Reviews of Environmental Contamination and Toxicology, v. 192, p. 117–158.

Saad, D.A., 2008, Agriculture-related trends in groundwater quality of the glacial deposits aquifer, central Wisconsin: Journal of Environmental Quality, v. 37, supp. 5, p. 209–225.

Sedmak, G., Bina, D., MacDonald, J., and Couillard, L., 2005, Nine-year study of the occurrence of culturable viruses in source water for two drinking water treatment plants and the influent and effluent of a wastewater treatment plant in Milwaukee, Wisconsin (August 1994 through July 2003): Applied and Environmental Microbiology, v. 71, no. 2, p. 1042–1050.

Snyder, S.A., Trenholm, R.A., Snyder, E.M., Bruce, G.M., Pleus, R.C., and Hemming, J.C.D., 2008, Toxicological relevance of EDCs and pharmaceuticals in drinking water: American Water Works Association Research Foundation, 121 p. plus 10 appendixes, available online at *http://environmentalhealthcollaborative.org/images/91238_Toxicological_Relevance.pdf*.

University of Wisconsin Extension and U.S. Geological Survey, 2007, Groundwater contamination susceptibility map, *in* Protecting Wisconsin's groundwater through comprehensive planning: U.S. Geological Survey, accessed June 21, 2012, at *http://wi.water.usgs.gov/gwcomp/find/door/susceptibility.html*.

U.S. Environmental Protection Agency, 2012a, Safe Drinking Water Information System, accessed June 22, 2012, at *http://water.epa.gov/scitech/datait/databases/drink/sdwisfed/index.cfm#1*.

U.S. Environmental Protection Agency, 2012b, Drinking water contaminants, accessed June 22, 2012, at *http://water.epa.gov/drink/contaminants/index.cfm*.

U.S. Environmental Protection Agency, 2012c, Where you live—Your drinking water quality reports online: U.S. Environmental Protection Agency Consumer Confidence Reports, accessed June 22, 2012, at *http://cfpub.epa.gov/safewater/ccr/*.

U.S. Environmental Protection Agency, 2012d, CCL and regulatory determinations home, accessed June 22, 2012, at *http://water.epa.gov/scitech/drinkingwater/dws/ccl/index.cfm*.

U.S. Environmental Protection Agency, 2012e, Source Water Assessments, accessed June 22, 2012, at *http://water.epa.gov/infrastructure/drinkingwater/sourcewater/protection/sourcewaterassessments.cfm*.

U.S. Environmental Protection Agency, 2009 National Lakes Assessment—A collaborative survey of the Nation's lakes: EPA 841–R–09–001, accessed July 3, 2012, at *http://www.epa.gov/owow/LAKES/lakessurvey/pdf/nla_report_low_res.pdf*.

U.S. Geological Survey and Michigan Department of Environmental Quality, 2003, Final draft of Source Water Assessment report for the City of South Haven water supply: Michigan Department of Environmental Quality, Water Division, Assessment Report 48, 18 p., accessed June 21, 2012, at *http://www.south-haven.com/pages/public_works/pdf/Source-Water-Assessment-Report.pdf*.

Wisconsin Department of Natural Resources, 2003, Source Water Assessment for Sheboygan water utility: Wisconsin Department of Natural Resources, 19 p., accessed June 21, 2012, at *http://dnr.wi.gov/org/water/dwg/swap/surface/sheboygan.pdf*.

Wisconsin Department of Natural Resources [n.d.], Arsenic in drinking water & groundwater, accessed June 21, 2012, at *http://dnr.wi.gov/org/water/dwg/arsenic/*.

World Health Organization, 1998, Cyanobacterial toxins—Microcystin-LR in drinking-water: Originally published in Guidelines for drinking-water quality (2d ed.), addendum to v. 2, Health criteria and other supporting information, accessed July 3, 2012, at *http://www.who.int/water_sanitation_health/dwq/chemicals/cyanobactoxins.pdf*.

Kites Over Lake Michigan, Lester Public Library

We Can All Swim in the Water

Importance of Swimming in the Water to Lake Michigan Communities

Lake Michigan has abundant beaches available for recreation, and 442 of them were monitored for recreational water quality in 2010: 24 in Indiana, 50 in Illinois, 78 in Wisconsin, and 290 in Michigan (*http://water.epa.gov/type/ oceb/beaches/seasons_2010_index.cfm#states*). Although there has been no systematic assessment of the importance of swimmable beaches, some examples indicate that beaches contribute profoundly to the economies of the States bordering Lake Michigan, and to the economic and physical well-being of their residents. One report indicated that in 1996, visitors to Indiana's counties bordering Lake Michigan spent over $523 million and that beach closures due to unsuitable water quality cost as much as $5 million per day in lost revenue (*http://www.great-lakes.net/humanhealth/lake/michigan.html*; Great Lakes Commission, 2003). Rabinovici and others (2004) estimated a net economic loss among potential swimmers of $1,272–$37,030 (depending on assumptions) for 1 day of closure at a Lake Michigan beach; these costs include the value of recreation and the cost of health effects.

Beach Monitoring

The frequency of Great Lakes beach monitoring and the consistency of monitoring targets have improved since passage of the Beaches Environmental Assessment and Coastal Health (BEACH) Act of 2000, which authorized the U.S. Environmental Protection Agency (EPA) to provide grants for monitoring and public notification to the marine and Great Lakes coastal States. In 2010, the EPA provided $960,000 in grants to the four States bordering Lake Michigan to implement beach monitoring and provide public notification. Currently, all States in the Great Lakes region, including those bordering Lake Michigan, monitor the majority of their priority beaches for the presence of *Escherichia coli (E. coli)*, a fecal indicator bacterium (FIB) whose presence in water has traditionally been assumed to indicate fecal pollution and, hence, the potential for detrimental human and animal health effects due to actual pathogenic bacteria, viruses, or protozoa. Only beach water—not beach sand—is tested. Beach monitoring results are typically made public through Web pages such as *http://www.deq.state.mi.us/beach/* for Michigan (Michigan Department of Environmental Quality, 2010). Each State also summarizes its yearly results for the EPA, and all reports are posted at the EPA Web site at *http://water.epa.gov/type/ oceb/beaches/seasons_2010_index.cfm* (U.S. Environmental Protection Agency, 2010a). In addition, the Natural Resources Defense Council (2011) publishes a yearly report that summarizes the State-provided data in different formats at *http://www.nrdc.org/water/oceans/ttw/titinx.asp*. Through initial funding from the EPA Great Lakes National Program Office (*http://www.epa.gov/greatlakes/about.html*; U.S. Environmental Protection Agency, 2012a) and subsequent funding from the Great Lakes Restoration Initiative (*http:// www.epa.gov/greatlakes/index.html*; U.S. Environmental Protection Agency, 2012b), beach managers have been encouraged to conduct sanitary surveys of their beaches as part of their monitoring efforts. In addition, the Alliance for the Great Lakes conducts a beach sanitary survey program, staffed by volunteers (Alliance for the Great Lakes, 2012), that has posted data from 2002 to the current date online at *http://www. greatlakes.org/adoptabeach*.

Identifying Key Processes and Uncertainties

Current monitoring programs for beaches are focused on periodic measurements of *E. coli* bacteria in beach water and are driven by regulatory mandates. Monitoring is typically carried out by various government health or recreation departments. Consensus is building that multiple complex processes, including those outlined below, need to be measured and understood before true protection of public health at beaches can be achieved (Dyble and others, 2008; Grant and Sanders, 2011; Zhu and others, 2011). Typical monitoring agencies do not have the scientific expertise, resources, or authority to investigate the geomorphic, hydrologic, or biological processes at the coastal/nearshore scale, which likely influence beach microbiological water quality and, hence, this Lakewide Management Plan (LaMP) goal. Although there has been much leadership within the Great Lakes research community on beach issues—particularly with regard to *E. coli* dynamics and the development of models that can predict when *E. coli* concentrations exceed standards—research on geomorphic and hydrologic processes lags quite far behind similar research for marine coastlines. We used the framework to outline the relevant processes; the following discussions are drawn from the example table, appendix 3.

Geomorphic Processes

Beach geomorphology includes the shape and dynamics of such features as dunes, interdunal areas, the swash zone, the shallow water table, and sediment transport along beaches—in other words, the factors that make a shoreline into a beach. Beaches take many forms in the Great Lakes, from flat and damp to high sand dunes with dry sands. The natural history of sand and gravel beaches and the types of beaches most likely to be used extensively by the public in Lake Michigan are profiled by the Michigan Natural Resources Inventory at *http://mnfi. anr.msu.edu/communities/index.cfm* (Michigan State University Extension, no date).

An extensive review of beach or coastal geomorphology is beyond the scope of this document. In any case, beach geomorphology has rarely been discussed with regard to the microbiology of beach water. Shoreline conditions throughout the Great Lakes are highly modified; for example, the south shore of Lake Erie is "severely sand-starved" compared to early settlement conditions, and almost 83 percent of that shoreline is hardened and protected from natural processes (Morang and others, 2011). Artificial embayments or structures that prohibit the natural flow of water along the shoreline may lead to concentration or focused deposition of bacteria-laden sediments (Ge and others, 2010). In municipal areas, it is not uncommon for sands to be brought to beaches and for a beach to be groomed, which changes the slope and type of beach materials. Beach-grooming methods affected *E. coli* concentrations at a Lake Michigan beach in Racine, Wis. (Kinzelman and others, 2004), and a relation exists between natural and degraded beach conditions and *E. coli* concentrations in shallow groundwater below those beaches (Crowe and Milne, 2007).

Hydrologic Processes

Hydrologic processes that influence beaches include those that affect nearshore sediments and sand, such as flow and sediment transport from river watersheds, creeks, and storm drains near or on the beach; runoff from the beach catchment (the area that contributes water directly to the beach during rainfall events); nearshore groundwater; longshore currents; interaction between nearshore and large lake currents; and waves. Hydrologic interactions between the open Great Lakes, the coastal boundary area, and the surf and swash zones were reviewed by Rao and Schwab (2007), who pointed out that we are "…still a long way from having predictive understanding of the dynamics of sediment, contaminant, and pathogen transport near beaches." A "beach boundary layer model" has recently been defined (Grant and Sanders, 2011) that incorporates contributions of FIB from bird droppings, shedding of FIB by bathers, dry sources, and wet-weather runoff from the shoreline, shallow groundwater, beach sediments, nearshore waters, and marine embayments. The model includes growth, entrapment, and resuspension of FIB in marine sediments and sands. A similar model was defined for a Florida beach (Zhu and others, 2011), and the role of coupled physical-biological models in addressing human health risk at marine beaches has been described by Dyble and others (2008). In Lake Michigan, circulation patterns in an embayed beach led to entrainment of FIB and subsequent influence on beach water quality in the knee-deep and swash zones (Ge and others, 2010). Models developed for predicting when *E. coli* may exceed water quality standards (Environmental Protection Agency, 2010b; Ohio Nowcast, at *http://www.ohionowcast. info/index.asp*) have successfully demonstrated that large-scale factors such as wind direction, wave height, and rainfall can be used to predict when *E. coli* concentrations will likely be high. Studies of beaches near large rivermouths have shown that rivers influence those beaches under specific weather conditions so that the river plume is directed to the beach (Nevers and others, 2008). All of these complex hydrologic factors may be operational at a given beach on a given day; however, the significance of each factor may vary from day to day. Nevertheless, there is no systematic effort to study, describe, and model the complex hydrologic and biological interactions that influence FIB and pathogens at Great Lakes beaches.

Biological Processes

The biological processes that influence beach water quality are generally associated with the presence of bacteria, viruses, and other pathogens in beach water and sand. Beach water quality is determined by the abundance of FIB, typically *E. coli.* An analysis for *E. coli* takes 24 hours to complete and, therefore, the test results refer to the quality of yesterday's water—a major limitation to protecting today's swimmers from health hazards. Additionally, the monitoring programs of the States that surround Lake Michigan vary substantially in the frequency with which beaches are monitored;

the monitoring program design may include the number of samples per beach, the timing of samples, and the depth at which samples are collected, and all influence *E. coli* concentrations and the policy choices regarding how and when to issue advisories or closures (Government Accountability Office, 2007; Nevers and Whitman, 2010). Even if the closure policy for a Lake Michigan beach could be implemented daily and without error, only about 42 percent of predicted illnesses would be avoided (Rabinovici and others, 2004). Possible reasons may include a lack of association between FIB and pathogens, spatial variability of FIB and pathogens that are not often accounted for, sources or pathogens other than water such as beach sand. Studies indicate that people swimming at Lake Michigan beaches influenced by human-sewage pollution contract gastrointestinal illnesses (Wade and others, 2006, 2008) and that the illness rate is related to enterococci concentrations, as measured by quantitative polymerase chain reaction (qPCR). Human viruses have been reported at some Lake Michigan beaches influenced by human-sewage pollution (Wong and others, 2009), and human viruses have been implicated as the disease agents in Lake Michigan epidemiologic studies (Soller and others, 2010). Finally, one study has shown that playing in beach sand at two Lake Michigan beaches was associated with gastrointestinal illness (Heaney and others, 2009), although beach sand is not monitored for microbiological quality (Halliday and Gast, 2011). At locations not influenced by an identifiable source of human sewage (nonpoint-source contamination), the likelihood of contracting illness and the relation of illness rates to FIB remains unknown (U.S. Environmental Protection Agency, 2009; Schoen and Ashbolt, 2010). Much recent research indicates that *E. coli* and other FIB, such as enterococci, may grow or persist in the environment or may be associated with nonfecal sources (Byappanahalli and others, 2003; Ishii and others, 2010) and, therefore, do not indicate fecal pollution when the bacteria sources are not fecal. On the other hand, FIB from wildlife may indicate significant potential for human illness (U.S. Environmental Protection Agency, 2009). Pathogens may also persist, or grow, in the environment, and many may have different survival characteristics than FIB (Dyble and others, 2008). Unfortunately, the sources of *E. coli* or other FIB, and certainly of pathogens, are rarely known. Among the four States bordering Lake Michigan, 85 percent of Wisconsin beaches reported unknown sources of *E. coli*, and Michigan, Indiana, and Illinois did not report any sources for 2010 (*http://water.epa.gov/type/oceb/beaches/seasons_2010_index.cfm#states*). Nationally, the National Resources Defense Council reported that between 2000 and 2010, over half the beach closure or advisory days were due to unknown sources of *E. coli* bacteria (National Resources Defense Council, 2011). The sources of the *E. coli* likely are unknown because current beach monitoring programs and sanitary surveys cannot capture the complex physical dynamics that bring source materials to the beach.

What We Know From Monitoring Efforts

The enhanced monitoring of Great Lakes beaches for *E. coli* bacteria that followed the BEACH Act of 2000, plus the implementation of sanitary surveys through EPA and GLRI funding, has improved our understanding of the locations and beach conditions where *E. coli* concentrations are frequently or persistently high. The enhanced monitoring has allowed sufficient collection of data to permit predictive models of when *E. coli* may exceed safe swimming standards to be developed for some beaches. Sanitary surveys have improved local beach managers' understanding of the factors that influence water quality at their beaches. In one case in Racine, Wis., better beach management—including modification of storm-drain outflows, planting of native beach vegetation, and altered beach grooming practices—has led to effective remediation of the causes of *E. coli* concentrations that exceed standards (*http://www.glslcities.org/best-practices/beaches/racine-beaches.cfm;* Great Lakes and St. Lawrence Cities Initiative, 2003). Unfortunately, most monitoring programs are not using enhanced methods, and monitoring programs largely do not focus on the sources of contamination. Most routine monitoring programs are not designed to address the geomorphic, hydrologic, or biological processes that underpin and influence health risk at Great Lakes beaches.

Knowledge Gaps and Uncertainties

One key uncertainty is the lack of epidemiological data for beaches (other than the select few that were chosen for their proximity to human-sewage influence) and a corresponding lack of actual pathogen data (except for a few limited studies). A second key uncertainty is fundamental knowledge on the primary sources of, and the processes that deliver, FIB and pathogens to Great Lakes beaches. Finally, as noted above, FIB are imperfect indicators of risk under all recreational-water situations. Although most beach managers and scientists could list an array of probable sources of FIB and pathogens for beaches, the degree to which any particular source plays a role at various types of beaches around the Great Lakes is unknown. Likewise, the geomorphic, hydrologic, and biological processes that deliver those FIB or pathogens to beaches remain poorly investigated. As a stark example, very few rivers in the Great Lakes are tested routinely, even for FIB; and if they were, very few river plumes and associated nearshore hydrodynamics have been successfully modeled in the Great Lakes (Rao and Schwab, 2007; Thupaki and others, 2013). Additionally, beach sands are an important contaminant source for beach water, and they have immediate health risks to beachgoers—but beach sands are rarely tested.

References

Alliance for the Great Lakes, 2012, Adopt-a-Beach™, accessed June 22, 2012, at *http://www.greatlakes.org/ adoptabeach*.

Byappanahalli, M.N., Whitman, R.L., Shively, D.A., Ting, W.T., Tseng, C.C., and Nevers, M.B., 2003, Seasonal persistence and population characteristics of *Escherichia coli* and enterococci in deep backshore sand of two freshwater beaches: Journal of Water and Health, v. 4, no. 3, p. 313–320.

Crowe, A.S., and Milne, J.E., 2007, Relationship between natural and degraded beach ecosystems and *E. coli* levels in groundwater below beaches of the Great Lakes, Canada, *in* Selected papers in hydrogeology—International Association of Hydrogeology Conference, Proceedings, Lisbon, Portugal, 2007.

Dyble, J., Bienfang, P., Dusek, E., Hitchcock, G., Holland, F., Laws, E., Lerczak, J., McGillicuddy, D.J. , Jr., Minnet, P., Moore, S.K., O'Kelly, C., Solo-Gabriel, H., and Wang, J.D., 2008, Environmental controls, oceanography, and population dynamics of pathogens and harmful algal blooms—Connecting sources to human exposure: Environmental Health, v. 7, supp. 2, article S5, 13 p.

Ge, Z., Nevers, M.B., Schwab, D.J., and Whitman, R.L., 2010, Coastal loading and transport of *Escherichia coli* at an embayed beach in Lake Michigan: Environmental Science and Technology, v. 44, no. 17, p. 6731–6737.

Government Accountability Office, 2007, Great Lakes—EPA and states have made progress in implementing the BEACH Act, but additional actions could improve public health protection: Washington, D.C., GAO–07–591, 44 p. plus 5 appendixes.

Grant, S.B., and Sanders, B.F., 2010, Beach boundary layer—A framework for addressing recreational water quality impairment at enclosed beaches: Environmental Science and Technology, v. 44, no. 23, p. 8804–8813.

Great Lakes and St. Lawrence Cities Initiative, 2003, Racine beach grooming tactics to reduce swimming bans, accessed June 21, 2012, at *http://www.glslcities.org/best-practices/ beaches/racine-beaches.cfm*.

Great Lakes Commission, 2003, Lake by lake—Michigan, accessed June 18, 2012, at *http://www.great-lakes.net/ humanhealth/lake/michigan.html*.

Halliday, E., and Gast, R.J., 2011, Bacteria in beach sands—An emerging challenge in protecting coastal water quality and bather health: Environmental Science and Technology, v. 45, no. 2, p. 370–379.

Heaney, C.D., Sams, E., Wing, S., Marshall, S., Brenner, K., Dufour, A.P., and Wade, T.J., 2009, Contact with beach sand among beachgoers and risk of illness: American Journal of Epidemiology, v. 170, no. 2, p. 164–172.

Ishii, S., Yan, T., Vu, H., Hansen, D.L., Hicks, R.E., and Sadowsky, M.J., 2010, Factors controlling long-term survival and growth of naturalized *Escherichia coli* populations in temperate field soils: Microbes and Environments, v. 25, no. 1, p. 8–14.

Kinzelman, J.L., Pond, K.R., Longmaid, K.D., and Bagley, R.C., 2004, The effect of two mechanical beach grooming strategies on *Escherichia coli* density in beach sand at a southwestern Lake Michigan beach: Aquatic Ecosystem Health and Management, v. 7, no. 3, p. 425–432.

Michigan Department of Environmental Quality, 2010, Michigan beaches, accessed June 22, 2012, at *http://www.deq.state.mi.us/beach/*.

Michigan State University Extension [n.d.], Michigan's natural communities, accessed June 21, 2012, at *http://mnfi.anr.msu.edu/communities/index.cfm*.

Morang, A., Mohr, M.C., and Forgette, C.M., 2011, Longshore sediment movement and supply along the U.S. shoreline of Lake Erie: Journal of Coastal Research, v. 27, no. 4, p. 619–635.

Natural Resources Defense Council, 2011, Testing the waters, available online at *http://www.nrdc.org/water/oceans/ttw/ titinx.asp*.

Nevers, M.B., and Whitman, R.L., 2010, Policies and practices of beach monitoring in the Great lakes, USA—A critical review: Journal of Environmental Monitoring, v. 12, p. 581–590.

Rabinovici, S.J.M., Bernknopf, R.L., Wein, A.M., Coursey, D.L., and Whitman, R.L., 2004, Economic and health risk trade-offs of swim closures at a Lake Michigan beach: Environmental Science and Technology, v. 38, no. 10, p. 2737–2745.

Rao, Y.R., and Schwab, D.J., 2007, Transport and mixing between the coastal and offshore waters in the Great lakes—A review: Journal of Great Lakes Research, v. 33, p. 202–218.

Schoen, M.E., and Ashbolt, N.J., 2010, Assessing pathogen risk to swimmers at non-sewage impacted recreational beaches: Environmental Science and Technology, v. 44, no. 7, p. 2286–2291.

Soller, J.A., Bartrand, T., Ashbolt, N.J., Ravenscroft, J., and Wade, T.J., 2010, Estimating the primary etiologic agents in recreational freshwaters impacted by human sources of faecal contamination: Water Research, v. 44, no. 16, p. 4736–4747.

Thupaki, P., Phanikumar, M.S., and Whitman, R.L., 2013, Solute dispersion in the coastal boundary layer of southern Lake Michigan: Journal of Geophysical Research: Oceans, v. 118, 12 p, doi:10.1002/jgrc.20136.

U.S. Environmental Protection Agency, 2009, Review of zoonotic pathogens in ambient waters: Office of Water, EPA 822–R–09–002, 75 p. plus 3 appendixes.

U.S. Environmental Protection Agency, 2010a, 2010 beach notification summary, accessed June 22, 2012, at *http:// water.epa.gov/type/oceb/beaches/seasons_2010_index.cfm.*

U.S. Environmental Protection Agency, 2010b, Predictive tools for beach notification, volume I—Review and technical protocol: Office of Water, EPA–823–R–10–003, 61 p.

U.S. Environmental Protection Agency, 2012a, Great Lakes National Program Office, accessed June 22, 2012, at *http://www.epa.gov/greatlakes/about.html.*

U.S. Environmental Protection Agency, 2012b, Great Lakes Restoration Initiative (GLRI) 2012 request for applications announced, accessed June 22, 2012, at *http://www.epa.gov/ greatlakes/index.html.*

Wade, T.J., Calderon, R.L., Sams, E., Beach, M., Brenner, K.P., Williams, A.H., and Dufour, A.P., 2006, Rapidly measured indicators of recreational water quality are predictive of swimming-associated gastrointestinal illness: Environmental Health Perspectives, v. 114, p. 24–28.

Wade, T.J., Calderon, R.L., Brenner, K.P., Sams, E., Beach, M., Haugland, R., Wymer, L., and Dufour, A.P., 2008, High sensitivity of children to swimming-associated gastrointestinal illness—Results using a rapid assay of recreational water quality: Epidemiology, v. 19, no. 3, p. 375–383.

Wong, M., Kumar, L., Jenkins, T.M., Xagoraraki, I., Phanikumar, M.S., and Rose, J.B., 2009, Evaluation of public health risks at recreational beaches in Lake Michigan via detection of enteric viruses and a human-specific bacteriological marker: Water Research, v. 43, no. 4, p. 1137–1149.

Zhu, X., Wang, J.D., Solo-Gabriele, H.M., and Fleming, L.E., 2011, A water quality modeling study of non-point sources at recreational marine beaches: Water Research, v. 45, no. 9, p. 2985–2995.

Sleeping Bear Dunes, Michigan Sea Grant

All Habitats Are Healthy, Naturally Diverse, and Sufficient to Sustain Viable Biological Communities

Importance of Healthy Habitats

Diverse habitat mosaics are found across the Great Lakes, and when healthy and well connected, these support diverse and productive biota. Healthy habitats provide suitable— and sometimes preferred—physiological conditions for the survival, growth, and reproduction of plants and animals. Habitats are composed of linked physical and chemical (dynamic) and structural (stationary) components (Peterson, 2003) that are created and sustained by both regional and local processes within a particular environmental setting or place. Habitats become limiting or impaired when their components become altered or the spatial connections among them become uncoupled in a way that reduces populations or causes local extinction (Schlosser, 1995; Schindler and Scheuerell, 2002). On a landscape scale or across neighboring habitats, impairments can result in system-level changes that increase the amount of (sink habitat (suboptimal, but accessible, habitat) relative to the amount of (source habitat (habitat that is optimal for reproduction or growth). Thus, population productivity is reduced if source habitat becomes limiting (Dunning and others, 1992).

Habitats and Their Structure

Here we use habitat in the sense of "place," delineated by patterns in physical processes and physical and vegetative characteristics. Combinations of variable hydrologic and geomorphic processes result in physical and chemical characteristics with distinct features that set the stage for biological habitat components (Hayes and others, 1996). Habitats are often usefully described as a nested series of spatial units (Frissell and others, 1986). Overarching processes such as climate, geologic history, and large-scale lake currents affect landscape composition. Large or macro-scale processes include distinct localized processes and physical and chemical features, such as localized climates, river or lake currents, or geomorphic landforms. Macro-scale processes give rise to predictable intermediate or meso-scale patterns in habitat complexity, patchiness, and diversity, such as pools and riffles in streams (see Peterson, 2003, and references therein). Thus, understanding ecosystem habitat health and restoration requires considering the processes that determine habitat quantity and quality across different habitat scales.

Great Lakes management programs have commonly emphasized aquatic habitats that are consistently or seasonally submersed. In this paper, for Lake Michigan, we have categorized aquatic habitats according to three ecosystem zones: (1) open lake, (2) coastal/nearshore, and (3) watershed (including tributaries). For Lakes Huron, Erie, and Ontario, we would also include a category of great connecting rivers. We explicitly include riparian terrestrial habitats within our coastal/nearshore and watershed zones, recognizing their dependence on and influence on neighboring aquatic habitats and importance to Lake Michigan ecosystem health. Connectivity among these zones contributes to ecosystem habitat diversity and function.

Habitat Trends

Noss and others (1995) considered the Great Lakes States among the 21 most endangered ecosystems in the United States. Lake Michigan has 10 Areas of Concern (AOCs) that have multiple impairments of beneficial use (Great Lakes Water Quality Agreement). The Great Lakes Restoration Initiative (GLRI) began in 2010 and is considered "the largest investment in the Great Lakes in two decades" (*http:// greatlakesrestoration.us;* Great Lakes Restoration Initiative, 2010). Urgent issues identified in the GLRI Action Plan include (1) habitat restoration focusing on toxic substances and areas of concern and (2) habitat and wildlife protection and restoration. The GLRI brought an increased focus to Great Lakes habitat issues and restoration needs; of specific importance is the coastal/nearshore zone, where much of the Great Lakes human population lives and works.

Habitat trends in the coastal/nearshore zone may have great influence on habitat in the other zones. Mackey (2009) stated "the single most important anthropogenic factor disrupting coastal/nearshore processes and pathways is increasing shoreline development and the physical alteration of the land-water interface." Cloern (2001) highlighted accelerated worldwide concerns about coastal eutrophication—the process of human mobilization of nutrients and other materials that are ultimately delivered to nearshore waters—resulting in excessive growth of aquatic plants and depletion of dissolved oxygen. Concerns about coastal eutrophication are fully applicable in the Great Lakes, as evidenced by current nuisance algal blooms. The Great Lakes currently are at a historic juncture for coastal management because earlier manufacturing-based coastal economies have become depressed in response to industrial life cycles and the national economy; thus, the region is potentially looking at a future period of redesigning, retrofitting, and redeveloping Lake Michigan's coasts. Many watersheds may face similar developmental histories and future trajectories that will create opportunities to consider ecosystem health as it relates to changes in hydrologic and sediment regimes, nonpoint-source loadings, and future human uses of the region's resources.

Identifying Key Processes and Uncertainty

Habitats arise from interactions between geomorphic, hydrologic, and biological processes. Thus, habitat restoration efforts for Lake Michigan should consider (1) how these processes structure or define habitat suitability, (2) how human activities influence these processes, and (3) how to devise and implement effective restoration activities that restore natural processes to provide healthy and diverse habitats. We used the framework to outline the relevant processes; the following discussions are drawn from the example table, appendix 4.

Geomorphic Processes

Glacial processes initially shaped lake depth and the form and texture of lake-bottom ridges, troughs, and plains. Such glacially sculpted patterns drive macro-scale processes affecting habitat character; for example, glacial ridges within the open-lake zone that provide shallow spawning reefs for native fish such as lake trout. Dynamic sediment-transport processes within the open-lake zone can influence localized bottom-sediment texture and sediment-exchange rates between coastal/nearshore and open-lake zones that may become increasingly important under high nearshore erosion conditions. Within the coastal/nearshore zone, glacial processes formed coastline shapes and textures that influence wave energy, sediment deposition and retention, and habitat suitability for aquatic biota. Glacial processes also resulted in coastline dunes and swamps that determine the composition and distribution of land-dwelling animals and plants. Glacial processes likewise shaped watersheds by influencing river catchment sizes, topography, sediment types, and valley structure. These effects carry over to determine valley-specific shape and sediment dynamics that influence erosion, transport, and deposition of sediments and nutrients and the accumulation of woody debris. Variability in land form and texture among and with tributary watersheds creates diverse aquatic habitat availability at the landscape scale; for example, Lake Michigan tributaries range from (summer) slow-moving, warm streams with sand and silt bottoms to swift-flowing, cold streams with gravel and cobble bottoms. Further habitat variability is seen within individual river channels, in terms of proportions of riffle (shallow, swift, and turbulent water over rocks), pool (deep and slow water), and run (mid-depth, smooth-flowing water) habitats found.

Anthropogenic modifications to the natural glacial shaping of the lake alter sediment dynamics such as loading, erosion, transport, and deposition across all zones. Human modifications to coastline shape, such as piers and breakwalls, can change shoreline currents and alter water- and sediment-exchange rates between rivermouths and open-water zones. Breakwalls that reduce water-exchange rates can result in effectively isolated eddies with high risk for bacterial concentration and toxic algal blooms. Furthermore, shoreline development that results in loss of coastal wetlands or natural-ized shore areas reduces habitat suitability and diversity to wildlife species including juvenile fishes that find refuge in the coastal/nearshore zone and migratory birds that utilize midwestern flyways.

Hydrologic Processes

Hydrologic processes influence habitat quality and diversity by determining flow sources of water to habitats, patterns of seasonal variations in water flow, and physical/chemical properties of water such as nutrient concentrations or water temperature. Large-scale currents and seasonal mixing of layers of lake water with different temperatures (stratification) influence nutrient availability for open-lake production, as well as water clarity and temperature regimes that are important to food availability. In winter, ice influences water strati-fication, and thermal and hydraulic refuges, and these effects carry over to spring production dynamics. Thermal habitat par-titioning has been observed for open-lake fish species (Brandt, 1980) and, thus, these hydrologic dynamics are important to open-lake habitat structure. Coastal/nearshore zone habitats can be especially dynamic because of storm surges, seiches, and upwellings that determine the stability of these habi-tats as well as nutrient delivery to plants for photosynthesis (Mortimer, 2004). This zone also encompasses lower energy habitats such as drowned lakes, wetlands, and bays. Hydro-logic processes within the coastal/nearshore zone are com-plex because exchanges occur between open-lake waters and watersheds. Tributary habitats are driven by instream flows, suspended sediments, nutrients, and temperature conditions, along with anthropogenic influences on watersheds and stream channels. These characteristics are highly variable across Lake Michigan tributary watersheds. Groundwater contributions are very important to Lake Michigan tributaries, accounting for 51–81 percent of annual streamflow to the lake (highest contribution among the Great Lakes; Grannemann and others, 2000; Neff and others 2005). Groundwater springs and seeps create localized thermal and water-quality refuges within streams across the basin, as well as within nearshore waters (Grannemann and others, 2000; Haack and others, 2005).

Anthropogenic alterations to hydrologic processes can set off a chain of effects that result in debilitation of habitat qual-ity. Air pollutants from inland sources can cause increases in airborne contaminant deposition to the lake and alter climates, thus changing seasonal thermal dynamics and ice conditions, which can result in spatial changes to species distributions or population reductions. Shoreline development alters the water exchange rate between the three ecosystem zones by re-directing wave energy and disconnecting coastal wetlands. Modifying landscape hydrology results in increased surface water runoff. Modifications at point locations within water-sheds, such as water withdrawals and reservoir construction, alter flow rates and water temperatures, which can influence migratory fish movements and spawning and rearing habitat quality.

Biological Processes

Biological and biogeochemical processes are important to habitat quality and diversity and to provision of food resources, hydraulic refugia, and predator refugia. Within the open-lake and coastal/nearshore zones, one key biological pro-cess is the accumulation and dispersal of woody debris, which settles to the bottom and thus provides important structural habitat and complexity (Maser and Sedell, 1994; Elosegi and Johnson, 2003). Within the coastal/nearshore zone, submerged and emergent vegetation provide some species with refuge from predators and support periphyton growth and localized food production. Macro-scale habitats within the coastal/nearshore zone can be quite variable in primary production because of localized temperature dynamics and nutrient loadings and, thus, provide differential quality habitat. Höök and others (2001) describe how macro-scale dynamics can structure habitat patchiness by highlighting that aquatic plants reduce the impacts of wave energy and alter local temperatures by reducing water circulation. Within these habitats, biogeo-chemical processes that drive nutrient and carbon cycling are important for biological growth and healthy diverse habitats.

Healthy and diverse habitats within the coastal/nearshore zone include riparian beaches, connecting wetlands, and the belt of shoreline development that influences habitat quality for terrestrial vegetation and wildlife. Important factors include seed banks and pollination dynamics for plants, structural cover for wildlife, and spatial distribution of habitat patches for aerial migrants. Terrestrial habitats in the coastal/nearshore zone also interact with aquatic zones, and this interaction has implications for fish, wildlife, and humans. For example, foreshore sand can act as an *Escherichia coli* source to Lake Michigan (Whitman and Nevers, 2003). Dynamic biological habitat drivers within the watershed include interactions with riparian flood-plain ecosystems and river-channel habitats; riparian complexity, such as the amount and quality of shading/canopy cover; and the accumulation of woody debris. Predation risk within the coastal/nearshore and watershed zones is influenced by influxes of nearshore spawning and anadromous fishes during spawning seasons, and by migratory bird populations. Connectivity among zones is critical to migrating fishes such as lake sturgeon (Smith and King, 2005) and for delivery of nutrients from watershed sources to open-lake habitats.

Anthropogenic effects modify biological processes influencing habitat quality; for example, human activities have modified the dynamics and distribution of woody debris in multiple ways. Today we see less large wood in river, river-mouth, and nearshore/beach habitats, because early 1900s logging removed the majority of older, larger trees and abun-dant dams captured most remaining wood that would naturally progress downriver to the lakes. And we are challenged by the large, underwater accumulations of polluting sawdust and debris that were deposited in rivermouths and bays by historical sawmills and other wood-processing operations. The introduction of quagga mussels has resulted in restructuring of the open-lake bottom by converting historically soft-sediment areas to a hardened bottom. Quagga and zebra mussels have influenced nearshore habitat by increasing water clarity and allowing the proliferation of *Cladophora* spp., a kind of green algae, at increasing depths. Nutrient additions within the nearshore zone have resulted in localized high algal concentrations that shade aquatic plants, and dredging has increased coastline slope, reducing suitable substrates for aquatic vegetation colonization. Within the watershed, modified riparian zones influence erosion rates and, thus, can cause siltation in historically suitable spawning substrates. Riparian alteration also influences shading from vegetation; thus, water temperatures may exceed lethal tolerances for some native fishes or could increase production capacity for warmer water fishes.

What We Know from Monitoring Efforts

Habitat monitoring is conducted as part of small-scale studies, including focused work within AOCs and also through basinwide assessment efforts. Small, localized studies typically fall in one or two cells within the framework matrix (appendix 4), and findings have not been synthesized more broadly. Some ongoing, basin-scale initiatives include the following studies.

1. The EPA State of the Lakes Ecosystem Conference (SOLEC) Indicators (*http://www.epa.gov/solec/*; U.S. Environmental Protection Agency, 2012), which do cover most geographic, disciplinary, and process aspects of our framework to some level and have been tracked for many years.

2. The Environmental Indicators of the U.S. Great Lakes Coastal Region (Niemi and others, 2006).

3. The Great Lakes Coastal Wetlands Monitoring Plan (Burton and others, 2008), which links coastal biological and hydrologic (water-quality) metrics to watershed and coastal landscape conditions.

4. The USGS Great Lakes Coastal GAP Analysis (Morrison and others, 2005).

5. Other ongoing lake regionalization efforts (E. Rutherford, National Oceanic and Atmospheric Administration-GLERL, Ann Arbor, Mich., personal commun., 2008) that are building fish habitat mapping and classification tools to aid coordination and interpretation of basin-level monitoring efforts (*http://ifrgis.snre.umich.edu/projects/GLGIS/index.htm*).

Therefore, habitat monitoring has provided snapshots of habitat condition in many of the zone-discipline cells of the ecosystems framework, sometimes across larger scales and sometimes consistently monitored through time. Collectively, we have our finger on the pulse of many habitat conditions across much of the Lake Michigan watershed. The impaired conditions of habitats across the basin have been cataloged, and the stressors within watershed and coastal zones have been mapped (Niemi and others, 2006; Wehrly and others, 2010; Esselman and others, 2011; Allan and others, 2013).

Knowledge Gaps

Despite all of the substantial collective effort to monitor habitats for Lake Michigan, we still lack information for some key zone-discipline cells within the framework, and we have only begun to examine the underlying processes, within and across the zone-discipline elements, to provide a true ecosystems-based understanding of aquatic habitats of Lake Michigan. We have especially not recognized nor focused on the process linkages between the discipline cells for geographic zones (table 1); highlighting the interzone and interdisciplinary linkages will advance our understanding of habitats within a systems context. For the most part, these efforts are distinct and not cross-walked, and so "what we know" is difficult to compile.

The binational State of the (Great) Lakes Ecosystem Conference (SOLEC) indicators framework is designed to broadly cover many habitat aspects. As an example use of our framework, a careful overlay of SOLEC indicators on the ecosystems framework would prove useful to identify potential coverage and linkage gaps.

References

Allan, J.D., McIntyre, P.B., Smith, S.D.P., and 19 others, 2013, Plea Proceedings of the National Academy of Sciences, v. 100, p. 372–377, *http://www.pnas.org/cgi/doi/10.1073/pnas.1213841110*

Brandt, S.B., 1980, Spatial segregation of adult and young-of-the-year alewives across a thermocline in Lake Michigan: Transactions of the American Fisheries Society, v. 109, p. 469–478.

Burton, T.M., Brazner, J.C., Ciborowski, J.J.H., Grabas, G.P., Hummer, J., Schneider, J., and Uzarski, D.G., eds., 2008, Great Lakes coastal wetlands monitoring plan: Ann Arbor, Mich., Great Lakes Coastal Wetlands Consortium, Great Lakes Commission, 238 p. plus 3 appendixes.

Cloern, J.E., 2001, Our evolving conceptual model of the coastal eutrophication problem: Marine Ecology Progress Series, v. 210, p. 223–253.

Dunning, J.B., Danielson, B.J., and Pulliam, H.R., 1992, Ecological processes that affect populations in complex landscapes: Oikos, v. 65, p. 169–175.

Elosegi, A., and Johnson, L.B., 2003, Wood in streams and rivers in developed landscapes, *in* Gregory, S.V., Boyer, K.L., and Gurnell, A.M., eds., Ecology and management of wood in world rivers: American Fisheries Society Symposium 37, p. 337–353.

Esselman, P.C., Infante, D.M., Wang, L., Wu, D., Cooper, A., and Taylor, W.W., 2011, An index of cumulative disturbance to river fish habitats of the conterminous United States from landscape anthropogenic activities: Ecological Restoration, v. 29, no. 1/2, p. 133–151.

Frissell, C.A., Liss, W.J., Warren, C.E., and Hurley, M.D., 1986, A hierarchical framework for stream habitat classification—Viewing streams in a watershed context: Environmental Management, v. 10, no. 2, p. 199–214.

Grannemann, N.J., Hunt, R.J., Nicholas, J.R., Reilly, T.E., and Winter, T.C., 2000, The importance of ground water in the Great Lakes region: USGS Water-Resources Investigations Report 00–4008, 14 p.

Great Lakes Restoration Initiative, 2010, Great Lakes Restoration Initiative action plan: 42 p., accessed June 21, 2012, at *http://greatlakesrestoration.us/pdfs/glri_actionplan.pdf.*

Haack, S.K., Neff, B.P., Rosenberry, D.O., Savino, J.F., and Lundstrom, S.C., 2005, An evaluation of effects of groundwater exchange on nearshore habitats and water quality of western Lake Erie: Journal of Great Lakes Research, v. 31, supp. 1, p. 45–63.

Hayes, D.B., Ferreri, C.P., and Taylor, W.W., 1996, Linking fish habitat to their population dynamics: Canadian Journal of Fisheries and Aquatic Science, v. 53, supp. 1, p. 383–390.

Höök, T.O., Eagan, N.M., and Webb, P.W., 2001, Habitat and human influences on larval fish assemblages in northern Lake Huron coastal marsh bays: Wetlands, v. 21, no. 2, p. 281–291.

Mackey, S., 2009, Nearshore physical processes, *in* Nearshore areas of the Great Lakes 2009: Environment Canada and the U.S. Environmental Protection Agency, State of the Great Lakes 2009 Reports, EPA 905–R–09–013, p. 108–112.

Maser, C., and Sedell, J.R., 1994, From the forest to the sea—The ecology of wood in streams, rivers, estuaries, and oceans: Delray Beach, Fla., St. Lucie Press, 200 p.

Morrison, S., Passino-Reader, D.R., Myers, D.N., McKenna, J.E., Stewart, J., Scudder, B.C., and Lohman, K., 2005, Great Lakes regional aquatic GAP analysis—Preserving biodiversity in the Great Lakes Basin: U.S. Geological Survey, Great Lakes Science Center Factsheet 2003–1, 6 p.

Mortimer, C.H., 2004, Lake Michigan in motion—Responses of an inland sea to weather, earth-spin, and human activities: Madison, University of Wisconsin Press, 304 p.

Neff, B.P., Day, S.M., Piggott, A.R., and Fuller, L.M., 2005, Base flow in the Great Lakes Basin: U.S. Geological Survey Scientific Investigations Report 2005–5217, 23 p. (also available at *http://pubs.water.usgs.gov/sir2005-5217/*).

Niemi, G.J., Axler, R., Brady, V., Brazner, J., Brown, T., Ciborowski, J.H., Danz, N., Hanowski, J.M., Hollenhorst, T., Howe, R., Johnson, L.B., Johnston, C.A., Reavie, E., Simcik, M., and Swackhamer, D., 2006 (ver. 1.1), Environmental indicators of the U.S. Great Lakes coastal region: Great Lakes Environmental Indicators Collaboration, Natural Resources Research Institute, University of Minnesota Duluth, Report NRRI/TR–2006/11 to the U.S. Environmental Protection Agency STAR Program, 121 p. plus CD.

Noss, R.F., LaRoe, E.T., III, and Scott, J.M., 1995, Endangered ecosystems of the United States—A preliminary assessment of loss and degradation: U.S. Department of Interior, National Biological Service, Biological Report 28, 83 p.

Peterson, M.S., 2003, A conceptual view of environment-habitat-production linkages in tidal river estuaries: Reviews in Fisheries Science, v. 11, no. 4, p. 291–313.

Schindler, D.E., and Scheuerell, M.D., 2002, Habitat coupling in lake ecosystems: Oikos, v. 98, no. 2, p. 177–189.

Schlosser, I.J., 1995, Critical landscape attributes that influence fish population dynamics in headwater streams: Hydrobiologia, v. 303, p. 71–81.

Smith, K.M., and King, D.K., 2005, Movement and habitat use of yearling and juvenile lake sturgeon in Black Lake, Michigan: Transactions of the American Fisheries Society, v. 134, p. 1159–1172.

University of Michigan, 2009, Great Lakes Environmental Assessment and Mapping Project: accessed June 22, 2012, at *http://www.snre.umich.edu/greatlakesthreats/.*

U.S. Environmental Protection Agency, 2012, State of the Lakes Ecosystem Conference (SOLEC), accessed June 22, 2012, at *http://www.epa.gov/solec/.*

Whitman, R.L., and Nevers, M.B., 2003, Foreshore sand as a source of *Escherichia coli* in nearshore water of a Lake Michigan beach: Applied and Environmental Microbiology, v. 69, no. 9, p. 5555–5562.

Appendixes 1–4

Appendix 1. Processes and components that impact the Great Lakes Lakewide Management Plan goal: We Can All Eat the Fish.

Disciplinary subsystem	Geographic zone		
	Open lake	**Coastal/nearshore**	**Watershed**
Geomorphic (Retention of contaminants)	Substrate adherence and leaching from substrate. Sediment composition and interstitial spacing that drives bioavailability via contaminant burial or resuspension.	Substrate adherence and leaching from substrate. Topography and hydraulics of lowest river-valley segment, embayment, and coastline influencing contaminant retention and exchange with open lake. Coastal sediment dynamics driving erosion, transport, and deposition of contaminants within coastal/nearshore habitats.	Watershed soils. Watershed area and slope. Substrate adherence and leaching from substrate.
Geomorphic anthropogenic	Siting of offshore spoil areas for contaminated dredging materials.	Piers and breakwalls modifying shoreline processes, and lake influence and contaminant exchange with rivermouths and embayments. Security of confined disposal areas to prevent reloading.	Channelization that modifies contaminant deposition versus dispersal to coastal/nearshore and offshore zones. Artificial reservoirs that store, transform, and potentially release contaminants and influence water-temperature regimes and other water-quality properties of tributaries.
Hydrologic (Loading and transport of contaminants)	Seasonal lake mixing that drives contaminant resuspension from sediments. Large-scale currents that drive contaminant and pathogen dispersion and deposition. Persistence within the system due to physical and chemical properties determining contaminant half-lives.	Seasonal lake mixing that drives contaminant resuspension from sediments. Large-scale currents, upwellings, and storm-induced surges that drive contaminant and pathogen dispersion and deposition. Persistence within the system due to physical and chemical properties determining contaminant half-lives. Groundwater flow and delivery of contaminants and pathogens.	Tributary flow regime driving instream dispersal and transport of chemicals and pathogens. Groundwater flows that contribute dissolved contaminants to tributaries. Surface runoff that may deliver or disturb sediments.
Hydrologic anthropogenic	Air- and precipitation-borne contaminants and chemicals.	Point-source runoff from industrial land use; infrequent accidental loadings. Seasonal and climatic nonpoint runoff from local urban and agricultural landscapes.	Point-source runoff from industrial land use; infrequent accidental loadings. Seasonal and climatic nonpoint runoff from local urban and agricultural landscapes.
Biological (Causing illness or disease)	Presence, survival, and reproducibility of pathogens.	Presence, survival, and reproducibility of pathogens.	Presence, survival, and reproducibility of pathogens.

Appendix 1. Processes and components that impact the Great Lakes Lakewide Management Plan goal: We Can All Eat the Fish.—Continued

Disciplinary subsystem	Geographic zone		
	Open lake	**Coastal/nearshore**	**Watershed**
Biological (Transformation of chemical contaminants)	Fish life history, foraging ecology, and metabolism.	Fish life history, foraging ecology, and metabolism.	Fish life history, foraging ecology, and metabolism.
	Methylation of mercury by bacteria.	Methylation of mercury by bacteria.	Methylation of mercury by bacteria.
	Bioaccumulation of contaminants due to compound properties.	Bioaccumulation of contaminants due to compound properties.	Acute and chronic (lethal and sublethal) toxicity from water- and sediment-related contaminants.
	Settling phytoplankton that carry adhered contaminants to benthic zone.	Acute and chronic (lethal and sublethal) toxicity from water- and sediment-related contaminants.	
Biological anthropogenic	Fishery practices determining targeted species and locations.	Fishery practices determining targeted species and locations.	Fishery practices determining targeted species and locations.
	Catalytic impacts of invasive species on bioaccumulation.	Catalytic impacts of invasive species on bioaccumulation.	Catalytic impacts of invasive species onbioaccumulation.

Appendix 2. Processes that impact the Great Lakes Lakewide Management Plan goal: We Can All Drink the Water.

Disciplinary subsystem	Geographic zone		
	Open lake	Coastal/nearshore	Watershed
Geomorphic (Retention of contaminants)		Substrate: inorganic sources (arsenic, metals).	Substrate adherence and leaching from substrate.
		Substrate adherence and leaching from substrate.	Watershed substrate.
		Topography and hydraulics of lowest river-valley segment, embayment, and coastline influencing contaminant retention and exchange with open lake.	Watershed area and slope.
		Coastal sediment dynamics driving erosion, transport, and deposition of contaminants within coastal/nearshore habitats.	Groundwater hydrogeology.
			Sediment dynamics.
Geomorphic anthropogenic	Atmospheric contamination.	Substrate adherence and leaching from substrate.	Altered sediment dynamics.
			Channelization and artificial reservoirs that modify contaminant deposition versus dispersal to coastal/nearshore and offshore zones
			Enhanced erosion
Hydrologic (Loading and transport of contaminants)	Seiche.	Currents that drive contaminant dispersion and deposition.	Tributary flow regime driving instream dispersal.
	Large-scale currents that drive contaminant dispersion and deposition.	Persistence within the system due to physical and chemical properties determining contaminant half-lives.	Groundwater flow paths.
	Seasonal lake mixing that drives contaminant resuspension from sediments.	Seasonal lake mixing that drives contaminant resuspension from sediments.	Overland flow, infiltration, and associated contaminant transport to surface-water and groundwater systems.
Hydrologic anthropogenic	Air- and precipitation-borne contaminants and chemicals.	Modified coastal hydrology.	Modified hydrology (drains, wetland removal, impervious surfaces).
		Placement of water intakes.	Water-well placement.
		Point-source runoff from industrial land use; infrequent accidental loadings.	Point-source runoff from industrial land use; infrequent accidental loadings.
		Nonpoint runoff from local urban and agricultural landscapes.	Nonpoint runoff from local urban and agricultural landscapes.
			Groundwater pumpage

Appendix 2. Processes that impact the Great Lakes Lakewide Management Plan goal: We Can All Drink the Water.—Continued

Disciplinary subsystem	Geographic zone		
	Open lake	Coastal/nearshore	Watershed
Biological (Causing illness or disease)	Development cycle of cyanobacteria	Development cycle of cyanobacteria.	Development cycle of cyanobacteria.
		Natural sources, such as birds and wildlife.	Natural sources, such as birds and wildlife.
		Survival and naturalization of fecal indicator bacteria and pathogens.	Survival, refugia, and naturalization of fecal indicator bacteria and pathogens.
		Differential transport and persistence of different microbes.	Differential transport and persistence of different microbes.
Biological anthropogenic	Boat and ship waste dumping.	Storm drains that deliver biological contaminants.	Manure application and runoff into nearby waters.
		Shoreline septic systems that deliver biological contaminants.	Failing or leaking municipal sanitary waste systems, combined-sewer overflows, and sanitary-sewer overflows.
		Human bathing as a source of pathogens or fecal indicator bacteria, or bathing activities that result in release of bacteria into the system.	Wastewater-treatment-plant effluent discharges.
Biological (Transformation of chemical contaminants)		Oxidation and reduction of chemicals and compounds.	Oxidation and reduction of chemicals and compounds.
		Chemical pollutant degradation.	Chemical pollutant degradation.
Biological anthropogenic		Storm drains and urban runoff that deliver contaminants.	Chemical use (fertilizers, road salt, pesticides, industrial chemicals, chemicals of emerging concern).

Appendix 3. Processes that impact the Great Lakes Lakewide Management Plan goal: We Can All Swim in the Water

Disciplinary subsystem	Geographic zone		
	Open lake	Coastal/nearshore	Watershed
Geomorphic (Retention of contaminants)		Topography and hydraulics of lowest river-valley segment, embayment, and coastline influencing contaminant retention and exchange with open lake.	Watershed substrate.
		Substrate adherence and leaching from substrate.	Watershed area and slope.
		Coastal sediment dynamics driving erosion, transport, and deposition of contaminants within coastal/nearshore habitats.	Groundwater hydrogeology.
			Sediment dynamics.
Geomorphic anthropogenic		Substrate adherence and leaching from substrate.	Altered sediment dynamics.
			Channelization and artificial reservoirs that modify contaminant deposition versus dispersal to coastal/nearshore and offshore zones
			Enhanced erosion
Hydrologic (Fate and transport of fecal indicator bacteria and pathogens))	Seiche.	Currents that drive contaminant dispersion and deposition.	Tributary flow regime driving instream dispersal.
	Large-scale currents that drive contaminant dispersion and deposition.	Persistence within the system due to physical and chemical properties determining contaminant half-lives.	Groundwater flow paths.
	Seasonal lake mixing that drives contaminant resuspension from sediments	Differential transport and persistence of different microbes.	Differential transport and persistence of different microbes.
		Dispersion and physical processing.	Overland flow, infiltration, and associated contaminant transport to surface and groundwater systems.
		Lake-groundwater interaction.	
Hydrologic anthropogenic		Modified coastal hydrology.	Modified hydrology (drains, wetland removal, impervious surfaces).
		Point-source runoff from industrial land use; infrequent accidental loadings.	Point-source runoff from industrial land use; infrequent accidental loadings.

Appendix 3.   Processes that impact the Great Lakes Lakewide Management Plan goal: We Can All Swim in the Water.—Continued

Disciplinary subsystem	Geographic zone		
	Open lake	Coastal/nearshore	Watershed
Hydrologic anthropogenic (*continued*)		Nonpoint runoff from local urban and agricultural landscapes.	Nonpoint runoff from local urban and agricultural landscapes
		Impervious surfaces in beach catchment.	
		Contaminated nearshore groundwater.	
Biological (Source and behavior of fecal indicator bacteria and pathogens)		Natural sources, such as birds and wildlife.	Natural sources, such as birds and wildlife.
		Survival and naturalization of fecal indicator bacteria and pathogens.	Survival, refugia, and naturalization of fecal indicator bacteria and pathogens.
		Cladophora growth and decay.	
Biological anthropogenic	Boat and ship waste dumping	Storm drains that deliver biological contaminants.	Manure application and runoff into nearby waters.
		Shoreline septic systems that deliver biological contaminants.	Failing or leaking municipal sanitary waste systems, combined-sewer overflows, and sanitary-sewer overflows.
		Human bathing as a source of pathogens or fecal indicator bacteria, or bathing activities that result in release of bacteria into the system.	Wastewater-treatment-plant effluent discharges.

Appendix 4. Processes that impact the Great Lakes Lakewide Management Plan goal: All Habitats are Healthy, Naturally Diverse, and Sufficient To Sustain Viable Biological Communities

Disciplinary subsystem	Geographic zone		
	Open lake	Coastal/nearshore	Watershed
Geomorphic (Structuring of spawning, rearing, and refuge habitats)	Glacial processes that shaped lake depth, and form and texture of lake-bottom terrain (ridges, troughs, plains).	Glacial processes that shaped topography and texture of lowest river-valley segment, delta, embayment, and coastline.	Glacial processes that shaped watershed size, topography, sediments, and valley structure.
	Sediment erosion, transport, and deposition dynamics influencing texture of lake-bottom sediments.	Coastal sediment dynamics influencing erosion, transport, and deposition of sediments within coastal/nearshore habitats.	Watershed- and valley-specific sediment dynamics driving erosion, transport, and deposition of sediments within channel and flood plain.
		Tributary dynamics influencing erosion, transport, and deposition of sediments within coastal/nearshore habitats.	Interaction among hydrologic regime, geomorphic (hydrogeomorphic), and wood-recruitment processes that create patterns in mesohabitats (pools, riffles, runs).
		Topography and hydraulics of lowest river-valley segment, embayment, and coastline influencing sediment retention and exchange with open lake.	
Geomorphic anthropogenic		Piers and breakwalls modifying shoreline processes, and lake influence and exchange with rivermouths and embayments.	Altered watershed and valley sediment dynamics (loads, erosion, transport, deposition).
		Physical hardening and structuring of rivermouth and embayment shorelines.	Diking and hardening of channel shorelines that reduces habitat complexity in channel and flood plain.
Hydrologic (Flow sources and regimes; water mass characteristics)	Seasonal lake mixing (both vertical and with nearshore), and large-scale currents influencing clarity, nutrient, and temperature regimes.	Lake storm surges, seiches, upwellings influencing clarity, nutrient, and temperature regimes.	Watershed-driven, tributary flow regimes driving instream clarity, nutrient, and temperature regimes.
	Winter ice-cover regimes.	Tributary inflow regimes influencing clarity, nutrient, and temperature regimes.	Hydrologic sources to riparian ecosystems (river floodwaters, groundwater).
		Dynamic hydrologic connectivity with coastal wetlands.	
		Topography and hydraulics of lowest river-valley segment, embayment, and coastline influencing water retention and exchange with open lake.	
Hydrologic anthropogenic		Piers and breakwalls modifying shoreline currents, and lake influence and exchange with rivermouths and embayments.	Modified watershed landscape hydrology (for example, wetland loss, urbanization, agricultural drainage) changing instream clarity, nutrient, and temperature regimes.

Appendix 4. Processes that impact the Great Lakes Lakewide Management Plan goal: All Habitats are Healthy, Naturally Diverse, and Sufficient To Sustain Viable Biological Communities.—Continued

Disciplinary subsystem	Geographic zone		
	Open lake	Coastal/nearshore	Watershed
Hydrologic anthropogenic (*continued*)	Air- and precipitation-borne contaminants and chemicals (acids).	Municipal and industrial wastewater discharges.	Point- and nonpoint-source inputs of contaminants.
	Climate change altering seasonal lake temperatures and ice regimes.	Nonpoint runoff from local or tributary watershed urban or agricultural landscapes.	Modified point hydrology (such as reservoir evaporation, dam release schedules, water withdrawals and diversions) influencing instream clarity, nutrient, and temperature regimes.
		Reduced hydrologic connectivity with coastal wetlands.	Development within flood-plain valleys that eliminates wetland services.
Biological (Food resources, and hydraulic and predator refugia)	Distribution and dynamics of floating and sunken wood debris recruited from coasts and tributaries.	Distribution and dynamics of sunken wood debris recruited from coasts and tributaries.	Stream channel interactions with riparian flood-plain ecosystems and river-channel habitats; effects on shading, bank structure, recruitment of woody structure.
	Distribution and dynamics of juvenile fishes produced in coastal/nearshore and tributary habitats.	Distribution and dynamics of juvenile fishes produced in open-lake, coastal/nearshore, and tributary habitats.	Instream dynamics of nutrient pulses in the form of fish eggs and fry (nutrients) imported from open-lake habitat.
		Dynamics of adult fish (predators) migrating from open-lake habitat.	Instream distribution of sources of primary production.
		Dynamics of aquatic and wetland macrophytes.	Dynamics of aquatic and wetland macrophytes.
		Distribution of sources of aquatic primary production.	
		Dynamics of terrestrial plants.	
Biological anthropogenic	Removal of dead trees; commercial log harvest.	Removal of dead trees; commercial log harvest.	Instream removal of dead trees; commercial log harvest.
	Restructuring bottom and altering nutrient pathways by nuisance dreissenid mussels.	Eutrophication-driven high algal concentrations shading bottom.	Modifications to riparian vegetation that effect flood-plain and channel habitats.
	Increased predation by hatchery-reared salmonids.	Increased predation by hatchery-reared salmonids.	Influx of hatchery-origin adult salmonids (predators) and their eggs and fry (nutrients) from open-lake habitat.
	Nuisance effects from accidental species introductions.	Nuisance effects from accidental species introductions.	Increased predation or nutrients from hatchery-reared, stream-resident trout.
		Removal of aquatic and wetland macrophytes.	Stocking of hatchery stream-resident trout, walleye, or other fishes.

Appendix 4. Processes that impact the Great Lakes Lakewide Management Plan goal: All Habitats are Healthy, Naturally Diverse, and Sufficient To Sustain Viable Biological Communities.—Continued

Disciplinary subsystem	Geographic zone		
	Open lake	Coastal/nearshore	Watershed
Biological anthropogenic (*continued*)		Elimination or disconnection of wetland habitats.	Nuisance effects from accidental species introductions
		Competition by nuisance terrestrial plants.	
		Impacts of feral beach nest predators.	

www.ingramcontent.com/pod-product-compliance
Lightning Source LLC
Chambersburg PA
CBHW080346290526

45791CB00009BA/2762

* 9 7 8 1 4 9 6 1 7 8 2 0 6 *